A QUEST THAT
IGNITES THE HEART

Also by Her Grace Archbishop Dr. Deloris Devan Seiveright

Hymnal & Trumpets—Shouter Spiritual Baptist (2000)
Thoughts & Prayers from the Heart (2001)
Rhythm and Soul CD (2001)
The Heart and Soul of Spiritual Baptist CD (2004)
Literature of Wisdom from the Heart (2006)

A QUEST THAT
IGNITES THE HEART

A Personal Journey

Archbishop Dr. Deloris Devan Seiveright

Order this book online at www.trafford.com
or email orders@trafford.com

Most Trafford titles are also available at major online book retailers.

Printed in the United States of America.

ISBN: 978-1-4669-1686-9 (sc)
ISBN: 978-1-4669-1687-6 (hc)
ISBN: 978-1-4669-1688-3 (e)

Library of Congress Control Number: 2012903224

Trafford rev. 02/21/2012

Trafford PUBLISHING® www.trafford.com

North America & international
toll-free: 1 888 232 4444 (USA & Canada)
phone: 250 383 6864 ♦ fax: 812 355 4082

CONTENTS

To Mom And Dad

PREFACE

You can know me by my words and way of life. *A Quest That Ignites the Heart* offers readers a heart-to-heart description of my journey—a country girl who grew up and learned how to excel in a big country. I have learned many lessons through my life, and I share them to empower readers and make you feel awesome. I would like those who read this book to feel the passion and let it reach their inner souls. The words should give them the answer to their problems and whatever decisions they have to make, because my story is somebody else's story.

I invite readers to share in my story of living, laughing, being happy, and knowing hurt, all with peace and love under a cloak of spirituality. I share my strength, tenacity, and rich, spiritual blessings to give hope and to invigorate readers with newness in life. Be ready to have your heart ignited and active with change. As you read, prepare for a new tomorrow, overflowing with success and blessings.

Thanks to my son Jezreel for adding a word or two and to my son Josiah for his positive thoughts. I do not have enough words to thank my daughter-in-law Maricia for her patience with me while she edited my writing. A special thanks to Keri, who also helped me. Thanks to my friend Harvey, who believed in me and said, "Get going! Just start writing. You have a lot to tell." Finally, thanks to John, who said, "Call the publishers now. Get it out there!"

A special mention for Nicole, Kimberley, and Michele, who came and helped me type this book. These three ladies also helped me with the organization to enhance the vision that was set for the community.

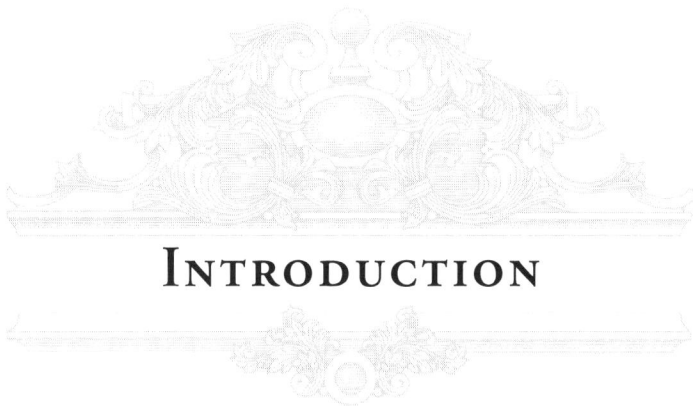

INTRODUCTION

I WAS BORN INTO a country home that was very quiet and peaceful with lots of fruits around for provision. The cane field, the pineapples, the garden, and the swing tree were awesome. The journey as I travelled the country roads to meet neighbours and go to school was amazing. Church had a pivotal role in my life; family was always around, and I had nurturing sisters and brothers. I also had great teachers, although they were very strict. I started working not only during summertime but also after-hours. I got my driver's licence when I was old enough, and when I drove down the dusty country road, the dust always blew in my face. The sun was so hot with raindrops on and off. There was excitement to prepare for church every Sunday. I watched Mama and Papa work hard to give us food.

Although I had a rich life as a child, this book will give you the knowledge of how I arrived from childhood to be a spiritual archbishop as a woman whose dreams were not focused on ministry. My life has taken a turn along a journey that I did not expect. In spite of the barriers and challenges, I have overcome and focused. Anyone who is able and willing will excel to do anything she puts her mind to. This journey is one of a kind and worth you knowing. I hope it will enrich your life as mine is enriched by God and by doing volunteer work and duties beyond my calling.

I am often asked why I am a Spiritual Baptist. People want to know how I went from being an Anglican in the Church of God to a Spiritual Baptist. When I reflect on my awesome journey, I am filled with spiritual joy. Over the years I have shared pieces of my story in articles I've written, interviews with students, lectures across North America and the Caribbean, and, of course, in front of my congregation on Sunday mornings. As an archbishop, I have travelled all over the world, received awards for my work as a community leader, and met fascinating people, but there were also stones and boulders on the path.

I regard the mercies and the blessings of God as an act of divine favour. His kindness and compassion have been extended to me, and His understanding surpasses human minds. He knows our failures and shortcomings, our sins, our infirmities, and our needs. I know for sure I approached God, and I have access to God's mercy. He blessed me, and He doubles the blessings when I show mercy to others.

My life was under the presence of these divinities. God is my guide; the angels are always looking after me, and God's divine direction leads me on daily. It was very hard for me to get around the spirit that engulfed my life but still be in the presence of work, school, family, and community. It was no problem, and it got hold of my daily walk as I was filled with joy and sadness, then love and a peaceful mind. It overwhelmed my heart, body, and soul. My friends, brothers, sisters, associates, and well-wishers, you too can feel the journey of your life as you read and feel the journey of my life—home-grown country girl to big city girl. I've experienced abuse, love, and family; I've worked in big organizations and received awards, accolades, recognition. And through everything I've had to focus on my humbleness.

Each chapter you read will give you a different experience. You will envision the journey and gain energy to prepare you for all challenges and success in your journey.

As a writer and a spiritual person who reads a lot, I put most of these stories in booklet form as I built new chapters and churches in Toronto. I have also trained and guided ministers with new ministries and supported the cause of the community spirituality.

My after-school routine started changing as I left for high school. I began to take music lessons from our church choir director. I would go to her home. She had a retail store and did a lot of baking. I would help in the store, and then when it was slow, she would teach me scales and notes.

I am devoted to the Spiritual Baptists. My devotion and message is from my heart. I embrace my spiritual journey with greatness; I wear my robes and my head wraps with pride. When I dance, I dance with God's power and greatness. I love music; I love to dance carnally, and so I love to dance spiritually.

I have a faith that embodies all faiths and that has a journey—a journey of development of peace and love and that portrays the indelible mark, the ancestors fought and left for us.

A student once asked me, "Why do you have all this passion and spiritual knowledge? What do you do?" I replied, "I have no choice. Yes, it is free will, but I am obedient. I was told by the Spirit, 'If you do not do God's work, you will be sick or may not live.'"

My mother is at an old age (ninety ninc). She exemplifies my deep spiritual roots from her birth. From a baby, she gave me that power and wisdom to be a spiritual person. I am a Christian by birth, but beyond that, I am a spiritual person who embraces all religions and believes all humanity is God's children. I believe in living pure, loving those around you, refusing hatred, and embracing forgiveness are the keys that matter. Therefore, I have work to do. I will do it; I cannot stop. I will preach, heal, and give direction in all that I do. Love is divine and supreme.

I always know that any male partner, who embraces me, if intimate, must be spiritual. If he is not, I cannot communicate in any such matter.

God used the storms in my life to strengthen my relationship with Him; if I put my trust in Him, I am safe, for He is my solid rock and safety in the storm. The journey in my daily life also leaves me with peace and calmness and gratitude. My spiritual life is a path for me, and no one else can walk it, only me, but there is support and guiding hands through the storms. Believing I was a superwoman, there have been storms in my life, but they have never lasted for long. They were only passing thunderstorms. I have often ignored storm watches and warnings, thinking that I could handle the storm by myself.

During college graduate school, I was married and had great sons, great parents, and great family, but I ignored the storm warnings. I collapsed emotionally. I had a fear of failure and believed that I had to be perfect. If I wasn't perfect, I couldn't love me, and then no one could love me, not even God. The stress of trying to do too much brought me to a breaking point. When I finally turned it all over to God, I was able to accept His unconditional love. Sometimes God allows me to use the spiritual gifts and talents to weather the storm. But sometimes in other storms, God asks me to leap the weather by faith into the water and swim for the shore. God speaks to me through His word, "calls upon me in the day of trouble, and I will rescue you if you honour me." Psalms 50:15

The Spirit had a mission yesterday, today, and in the future. I have founded and established a church, the people's church. I have compassion and empathy, and I know the Spirit will direct where to build and plant the churches, for the Spirit guides will show me the path.

I will do for myself as I do for others. I will talk east and walk east for sustainability for all is income, health care, education, and justice. The education that I need is spiritual and moral; all people deserve this, especially the youth.

Today when God calls you, harden your heart; if there is work for you to do, He will use you. God bless you. I will endeavour to ask the Lord to teach me in the way of His statutes, and I shall keep it until the end.

It was a very cold winter night when I prayed for a change in my life. I was about forty-eight years old. Within three weeks, an awesome turn came out. My career changed, and one of the things I will do and must do is to tell my stories, real stories, by television, radio, somewhat by teaching, preaching for sure, but certainly in book form. A dear friend, a lawyer, would always say to me, "Do not say you are going to write; just write." Also, another dear friend of mine, a judge, confirmed the same advice when he said, "You have so much to tell; just *tell it*."

I hope this book will enlighten you as my faith enlightens and empowers my life. Enjoy every word; it is real in my life. All my purpose, as well as the future, is all because God has been in the centre of my life. Thanks to my father and mother who taught me very well.

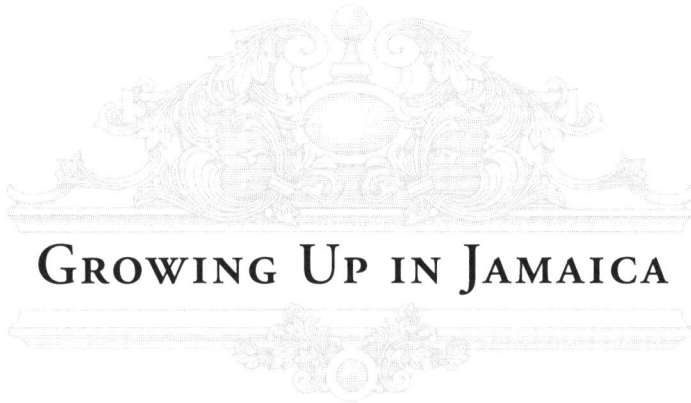

GROWING UP IN JAMAICA

" WE WERE BORN on the 26 of June 1948, he before me. Apparently, she lay down on my nose; hence I look different from her. By the way, she also suppressed my weight, as I only weighed two pounds at birth. Growing up she was pampered by our father. He taught her to drive the brand-new car, while I could only clean it or steal a drive. She was given the best room, went abroad to study and work instead of us or me. It's a good thing we were born together; we are still together in heart and soul. I love her more than myself." (Dennis Joan Seiveright, my twin brother)

From the beginning, life was full of surprises. My birth was a story unto itself. Every time our family meets the story is told with laughter and a lot of chat. It goes like this: I was born in a small town in Jamaica, the last girl, ninth from a family of eleven children, and the first of a set of twins. Mama did not know there was a second child coming. I was born first, and then the midwife announced, "There is another child coming. The girl is sitting on his nose. He is a boy, and he cannot breathe." Dennis was slapped several times, eventually breathed, and survived. Hence, the family joke of why Dennis's nose is flat.

Love your father; love your mother. Cherish every moment you spend with her; spend time with your parents. Both of them made a difference in my life. My mother's name is Alice. She was a prayer warrior. We called her Mama. I can recall getting up early every Sunday morning to the voice of Mother's prayers praying for all of us and calling each child by name. Some mornings we would kneel around my parents' bed, hoping and wishing that the prayer would be over in five minutes, but this was just a thought. Mama would go on until she was ready to go in the kitchen to get the roast beef, chicken, or fish ready. Her voice was like that of an angel. She loved to sing, and we all listened.

My father Conrad, who we called Papa (Mama called him Con), studied the Bible daily. He was a brilliant man, kind but firm. At home during dinnertime, Papa always started the conversation at the table. He would ask two questions. The first being, "What was the day's lesson at school?" The table rule was that while we were eating, we did not talk. As soon as we finished the last mouthful, we had to provide a detailed answer. For example, we would start by mentioning that we got into class before the bell. I would report that the teacher, Mrs. John, sung the song "New Every Morning Is Thy Love," and we followed. Then Papa would ask, "What about the schoolwork?" I would state that we had arithmetic, it was hard, and I did well.

The next question would always be, "Do you know who God is?" We had to answer with a scripture, and the text from the Bible must be correct. If not, he would point out that we needed to listen, learn, and retain information. It was always after this that Papa would preach and teach for the next hour. Mama would always have to interrupt him, pointing out that we had homework and needed to get ready for bed. Papa was very strict and watched over us like we were little chickens. This was the routine for many years. We had to practice what my dad and mom preached.

My daddy was the only one with a car in the area. So on our way to church, Papa (known by the people as Head Man or Mr. Con) would squeeze us up in the car, overloading it to carry people who would otherwise be late to church. The people were always humble and appreciative, saying, "Thank you, sir. God bless you, Mr. Seiveright, Head Man." The people respected and looked up to Papa like a role model within the community. Our family was one of a kind in the little town. We always talked about school and church and how Mama and Papa helped the people in the town.

I loved Dad too. He grew to be such a successful man and took his rightful place in his society. During my time away at school, Papa worked hard as a farmer to earn enough to send us to school. I recall him telling Mama that he would have to kill a cow to pay for my boarding and buy school books for the next term. My father was a deacon of the New Testament Church of God in Clark's Town, Jamaica. He was a very active person in not just his church, but also in the Anglican Church, as well as the community overall. He always made me laugh. He was funny and witty, a gracious man of God, and together with my mother, he cared for us and our neighbours. I remember him taking the neighbour to the hospital at two o'clock in the morning.

Someone would come calling, "Mr. Con, Head Man, it's Mrs. G, sir. We need a drive to the doctor."

He would get up and drive them to Dr. F, the town doctor. Like my father, Dr. F would get up at any time of the night or day to serve the community. When Papa came back home, he would say, "She is lucky to brut. If I did not take her, she would be dead, and we would be going to funeral." Mama would correct him, but he would just laugh and say, "Well she is home and good now."

Dad also loaned people money if needed or create jobs around the farm for them to do. Mama and Papa were two great characters. I never heard them fight or have a big fuss.

Our home at Hyde was a peaceful haven, and all the neighbours respected the Seiveright family. They all came up to get water, milk, ice, meat, yams, and pineapples—everything from our farm. There were even times when Mom had to dress or put bandages on people's cuts or sores. I recall the average day like this: Mama would pray and then have breakfast. A voice would come from down the road, saying, "Hold dog. Hold dog."

Mama would go to the veranda and say, "Oh, who is that?"

The person responded, "It's me, Miss Alice. I want to know if you have any ice or milk."

Mama would invite them in, saying, "Come, come. I will give you the ice and milk, but only one small bottle, because others still have to get some, and please remember to bring back my bowl to me to make more ice."

The lady got her milk and ice and headed down the road. By lunch time, food was ready, and the morning's visit would be repeated by someone else. My sister Daphne could see who was coming and made sure to hold onto our yard dog. Some needed medicine, while other's needed prayer.

Mama would always say, "Darling, let me see what I can do. Just pray, and I will too." She would get the herbs, put the food together, and send you on your way with a package. By evening, Mama may have had a few more visitors to our home. It was a walk-in clinic and drop-in food mart. It was a joy to see my mother, Miss Alice, doing what she had to do for her community.

The brothers and sisters I grew up with were very happy. We laughed and enjoyed time together as a family. We had a really happy family life. My advice to you is that if you need to be successful, stay your course, listen to your heart, spend family time together, and try to be at peace at all times if possible. Love your family and care for them daily. We knew Mama was at home working for us while Papa worked on the farm and around the home. They prayed, helped people, and provided us with great food, shelter, and a great home.

Dennis, my twin, stayed home working and was dedicated to this cause. He was always very funny. A great man, he chose not to leave home or travel abroad. Clover was a sister I knew very well; she was a smart, hard-working woman. Papa gave her a hard time, but she excelled very well. Clover lived in Kingston then made a beautiful career for herself in the United States. My oldest sister Daphne was like a second mother to us. She helped Mama around the home. Daphne made sure that we were all fed, our clothes were ready for school, and our beds were well made. She did the laundry and kept the floors spotless. She taught me how to clean, wash, and cook. I felt great love from her. In her eyes, I could do no wrong. She was very hard working and never talked too much, but when she did speak, you had better watch out, because she said everything from the heart. My brother Franklyn travelled all over. He later came to live and die in Canada. Rest in peace, Brother.

After supper and homework, we often had time to tell stories. One of the stories we told was about a man named JJ. He had died, and all the people in the town were afraid to travel during the dark of the night. The only people who were not afraid were the church people coming from Church of God or Gospel Hall or those meeting in the square. Well, everyone would pair up or walk very quickly and quietly from the town to Hyde, repeating, "The Lord is my Shepherd" and the rest of Psalm 23 until they reached home.

One night returning from church, Daphne said, "My head grew big. It must be JJ the duppy."

Mama said, "Girl, stop that! Just pray and keep saying the Lord is my Shepherd or the Lord is my light."

Daphne said, "But, Mama, I heard something in the road."

Mama said, "Girl, stop!"

Daphne said, "Yes!"

As they turned the corner in full speed, they saw a man in white robe coming out of the cane field. They ran so fast, it was as if they were running to win a race. They prayed and loudly said the "the Lord is my Shepherd." They ran up the hill, pushed the door open, and were out of breath. They got into the living room and dropped their Bibles on the floor. Their bodies were in shaking position, and they just dropped all their strength on the sofa and the chairs. Papa came out from his room into the living room and said "What is wrong? What is wrong? Alice, Daphne, what is wrong?"

Daphne could hardly catch her breath. "We . . . saw a man. It must be a duppy in a full white robe, down the road coming out of the cane field."

Papa laughed and laughed and laughed and said, "You guys must be still in spirit."

"No, Papa, my head grew big, and then the man came out the cane field and disappeared . . . disappeared in the road."

Papa laughed hard before asking, "Where is Franklin?"

Then Franklin walked up the road very calm and cool. Daphne said to him, "Did you not see the duppy?"

Franklin said, "What Duppy? No, well, I saw you guys running so hard I wondered myself."

"Where were you?" Daphne asked.

"I was waiting for you all, covered in a white sheet," he answered.

Well, Papa lost it. He took the belt and ran Franklin down in the dark, down the road and locked the door. "Why did you do that to the church ladies, your sister, and your mom?" Papa asked.

Franklin thought it was funny, but it wasn't funny to Papa. Papa usually drove them home, but they had decided that night that they wanted to walk home, because it was so nice out. The night turned out to be scary and could give them heart failure. The next day, everyone was told about the story, and we laughed, but with great sympathy for the church ladies and mom. This was my favourite story growing up.

Calvin, the youngest of us, continued school at William Knibb Memorial High School, the same school that I attended in Falmouth. He came to live in Canada as well. Although most of us children grew up and moved away, our home was never a lonely place. There were lots of grandchildren growing up in the home with my parents. Everyone knew their place. Respect was ever-present from the helpers right up to Papa. Prayer time, family time, and visiting time were all respected.

Our family was very big, but I grew to see most of my brothers and sisters leave home. They went to various parts of the world. My brother Keith went off to England, Madge was married in Kingston, and Cecile was in Brownstown. Cecile eventually moved to Canada from England, and when I left Jamaica to go to Canada in 1969, I did not know her very well, because she was always away from home when I was small.

Neville, our oldest brother, was a police constable in Ocho Rios, Halfway Tree, and then Clark's Town. My other brother, Malcolm left for Missouri to attend Bible college. He came back and became an evangelist and then left again to be an American. Boy, when Malcolm preached, you trembled, and he always brought down the crowd. He was one of the great Evangelists of the sixties and seventies. He was my model as a preacher. He studied well and had spiritual gifts of healing and a true prophetic voice. If Malcolm told you that rain was coming or that you should not go down to the garden because it wasn't safe, it was an accurate message from God through my brother. This is a gift that I can attest to and relate to in my everyday life. Trust me; it is a great experience to have a prophetic voice. Malcolm was a great, gifted speaker. May he rest in peace.

My brothers and sisters had to make up games and enjoy the day. My favourite games were skipping rope and hopscotch. In the country, I did not have the privilege of having dolls, watching TV, or listening to the radio. So, I made my own games. My grown-up years were focused on church, books, and games. During my childhood, I owned a pet named Pally, a brown dog. It was a protector for us coming home and at the home. As I take a moment and see the pictures of the home, our home was a home of happiness. Once we were home, it was a praying home, a singing home, and a laughing home. This story always stays with me. This other story reminds me of my cat.

We had a cat in the home that ran around and caught rats outside. My dad told us not to feed the cat too much, because he would get lazy and not want to eat the rats. Due to the cane field, there were always rats around the house. So we knew the cat would get them before they came inside. If Papa saw the cat inside, he said, "Go outside, you lazy cat! Go and work and catch the rats!"

One Saturday morning I was ironing while my sister and the helpers were cleaning. I was not good at ironing, because my sister and the helper were always doing it; however, as a lady in the house, I must learn to iron. So, there was a chance to prove myself in ironing. I remember the iron dropped off the ironing board. The iron was very hot. It fell on the cat beside my feet.

"Mama, the cat!" I screamed. Mama came in and took the cat, trying to revive it. I wish I remembered the cat's name now, but I do not. The sad news came to me that I had killed the cat. I cried and cried and cried until everyone had a little sympathy for me, after they had more sympathy for the cat first. From that day on, I would not go close to a cat or own a cat. By the way, I am allergic to cats.

Sundays were always my favourite day of the week. In the morning, the chickens would be clucking, the dogs would be barking, and the birds would be singing. You could feel the morning dew coming from the grass and the sunshine was cool. It was a refreshing day and time to get up and get ready for church. Some bathe outside, and others bathe inside. I put on my Sunday best, a nice dress and shoes.

Our Sunday breakfast would be ready by the time we were dressed. We all sat around the long dining table, seven or more of us, depending on who was home at the time. We enjoyed green banana, salt fish, ackee, and dumplings. Our eldest sister would make sure we ate and all sat quietly in the living room until Mom and Dad came out from their room all dressed in their best. Sometimes we would have to walk two miles to church if Dad was not ready in time for us to get to Sunday school. Only if he was going to adult Sunday school would we get a ride in the car. I loved Sunday school; it was a joy during my childhood days. As a child, I really enjoyed attending church with the singing and the people under the power of the spirit. My brothers would usually come home and re-enact how the ladies and my mom performed.

My father was one of the influential leaders of the church, my mother was the treasurer, one of my brothers was a pastor/evangelist, and the rest of my family who lived at home were Christians, the ones who were called true believers of Jesus Christ. Both of my parents prayed with their voices so loud that you could stay down the road and hear them. As a young child, I always thought that Mom and Dad had to pray loud because God was so far away. I also thought His answer to all of our prayers came to us through big successes.

As a little girl, I loved church. I was raised in the church, baptized at the age of twelve, and started organ lessons and singing in the junior choir at age thirteen. My spiritual quest started evolving around age twelve. I can recall being able to see, hear, and feel the next moments of my life and in the lives of people around me. I also can put my hand on someone, and where they have a pain, it will go away. I was a little girl with an old spirit I've been told. I was never afraid of the dark or to be alone. I was always afraid to comb my hair because of the time it took and the amount of people that had to be around me. As I mentioned earlier, I was always under the influence of Spirit, Angels, Spirit Guides, Holy Spirit, God's power, and the Holy Ghost—whatever you call this greatness.

I love school, and I study well. My favourite subject was literature. William Shakespeare's *Twelfth Night* and selections from Tennyson's *Collections of Great Poems* and *Work Tells the Story* were some of my favourites. In secondary school, I got an A in religion and literature. My next favourite was music, which is why I love Shakespeare. "If music be the food of love, play on."

For me, every morning was a dress rehearsal before I went to school. I would wake up at five o'clock every morning to Mama's praying, and then it was time to dress. Even at a young age, I took pride in everything that I did, especially my appearance. My dresses were always pleated, thanks to my sister Daphne or the helper (maid) who washed, starched, and ironed my uniforms. My school uniform was a turquoise-coloured skirt with pleats all around. The starch kept the pleats in place. I was really happy when I started wearing skirts. When you were a prefect student, you got to wear skirts, so I worked hard toward becoming the prefect student in order to wear skirt.

I walked two miles to school on dusty roads, taking care not to dirty my dress, and I always arrived when the bell rang. In order for my shoes to last, I walked barefoot with the shoes in my hand. When I was close enough to school, I used a rag that I carried to clean my feet and then put my nice, clean shoes on. When I sat down, I took the time to sit down slowly, placing my hands at the back of my uniform to ensure that the pleats were in place and not crushed. The high school I attended was thirty miles far away from home. Papa drove me and picked me up most of the time. Driving in our van was like gold. I say this because during this time in the country, most families did not own a vehicle. I always slowly placed my bum in first, followed by my two legs to make sure that

I entered the van like a lady. I have carried this care of my appearance throughout my whole life.

In the afternoon when school was over, my friends, brothers, sisters, and I would walk home together, calling out to all of our elders as we went by. "Good afternoon, Mrs Green. Good afternoon, Mr Jones," we would say. Our community believed in the tradition of a village raising a child. In order to prevent someone reporting to our father that we lacked manners, we made sure to call everyone by his or her name and title when passing by on the way home. The school day was over, and it was time for home and homework.

When I reached home, I had a routine. I took my uniform off right away and hung it up to wear the next day unless it was soiled or I was going to change it. If my pleats were crushed, I would iron them again. Then it was time for homework and something to eat.

Secondary school was thirty-two miles from home. During my secondary school days, I had to board and live away from home, because of my parent's beliefs in the Church of God doctrine.

Despite my excitement, my time away turned out to be another surprise in my life. Living with a minister and his family, I woke at five o'clock every morning to pray and had to be at church every night, even if I had homework. I also had to do all of the household duties. Supper was a small plate of food that would not even satisfy a cat. The fried dumplings were as small as a green lime, and I got only two each morning. I was not used to this. So in order to survive, I had to go to school with my pocket change and buy chocolate. The minister's wife did nothing and treated me like I was her servant. I would have to clean and iron constantly, often having to stand up and iron twelve white shirts for her husband all at once. Every weekend the minister and his wife would give a weekly report to my parents, and the lies they told about me would make tears come to my eyes. This was the first time I doubted the faith I had been raised in.

When I returned home at the age of sixteen, I had experienced a lot and wasn't sure that living my parents' Christian life would take me to heaven. By the time I turned seventeen, I was closely watching the lives of the church patrons, especially the deacons and ministers, and had made up my mind. The examples of Christianity I had encountered turned me away from wanting to live a Christian life. Before I reached the age of twenty-one, guess what? Church was no longer a priority anymore. I just wanted to socialize, party, and dance the night away. I continued to live my life, making my own decisions. I chose to disobey one of the church's man-made laws and wear pants. As per Deuteronomy 22:5, "A woman must not wear anything a man wears." Thus, it was a sin for me to wear pants. A meeting was called with the leaders, and I was crossed out of the church's record book. Now I felt like a real sinner. Confused about all of this, I asked the Lord to teach me the right way and show me His path.

The way they crossed my name out of the church was sad for me. Why? Because I thought I was crossed out of heaven as well. They saw me dressed in pants on the street in town and saw my hair permed. I was lost and did not obey the man-made law. Confused as I was, I reflected during my time of confirmation, and it was so gracious. I was in full white. The priest's wife, Prong, was my godmother. She was an English lady who treated me with great respect. I also remember being baptized at the age of twelve in the open pool in front of the church. I wore full white then also. These moments of happiness are memories I will always remember. I will always honour them, and I know that I was blessed. The name that was crossed out was sad, but I overcame with my inner spirit, and I recognize a few months later that I was truly a child of God. In no way was I out of God's books. This story, I am sure, can apply to many young people, but as a young lady, the testing will show how brave and how strong you can be.

When I had finished high school, Daddy gave me three options: attend nursing college in Jamaica or abroad, go with the missionary to Missouri for Bible college, or find a job until I decided what I was going to do. I found a job—a very good job. Working was very exciting for me. I was excited about making money. I drove my father's car to work and felt as though I was on top of the world.

I worked at Long Pond Estate where I met great people who helped me along the way. This job was during summer break and after I'd graduated from high school. My job was awesome. There I learned to be a receptionist, handle petty cash, and greet people from all over the world. My next job at Rose Hall was a good way to broaden my experience and gain maturity. I lived in the hotel residence. The other girls in my dorm were helpful and taught me how to manage my shifts and the tourists at the Half Moon Hotel at Rose Hall. One day at work I met an evangelist who wanted to take me to Bible school. I said, "No way!" I was oblivious about the future, not knowing about the life ahead of me or what God had in store for tomorrow.

When I started working as a youth, I had great confidence in myself. While I was working, I got a few hours training, and then I was on my own. I can recall the manager coming in on my afternoon shift. He said, "Watch me. This is the machine. As the guests come in, take their names, register them, give them the keys, explain their rooms and rules with deposits, and at the end of the evening, balance all deposits and put them in the safety deposit box. Then at check out, give them the bill and explain any miscellaneous charges." This took two hours with one guest, and I was on my own after that. I was very, very, confident. The next guest thought I was experienced and wanted to give me a tip, but I was not allowed to take tips because I was not the room maid or the waiters. My job was different anyhow. I met great people from England, the United States, and Canada, including lots of celebrities. I can assure you that I had no fear when I worked late until midnight. When I was done, I locked up the office and walked to the staff residence.

My Papa really loved me. I cannot deny that I was a spoiled child, but I had great respect for my parents. So before I disobeyed and decided what I wanted to do, I decided that I would travel. I left home and went to Canada to study and work. I owe a special thanks to my sister for sending for me.

The day I left Jamaica was a bright and sunny day the 24 of April 1969. The pastor came up to our home with a van full of church members to pray for my safe travel. They still insisted that I repent for my previous sin and said they had forgiven me like Jesus, seventy times seven. My father's advice was that when I reached Canada, I should get a good education. My brother's advice was that I should not marry any white men. The list went on and on about the things I should or should not do. From the airport balcony, they could all wave. I wore my pantsuit to the airport. I could see the crowd of people waving to me as I entered the plane. I felt like the queen of England. I boarded an Air Canada plane, and my destination was the Toronto International Airport.

The joy of sharing my life story with you plunges me into a state of introspection. I delve into my thoughts in my late nights with no time to spare, and yet, I have not shared the half of it. I have been writing for more than three years. My life's journey is to do the work I have to do here, because I am placed here for a purpose. In life, some may plan to be a doctor, a teacher, a business person, but when the plan of your life says "go to Canada and do the work of the ministry," that is the call.

BUILDING A LIFE IN CANADA

I ARRIVED IN TORONTO and was met by two ladies at the airport who said they were my sister Cecile's friends. Cecile was busy at work and could not meet me at the airport. Wow! Wow! Wow! I had no Mummy and Daddy, no church members, nobody who knew me. There was just my sister who was too busy for me, because she worked night and day. She was a nurse with a busy schedule and crazy hours, so she had arranged to let her friends take me around. I had forgotten that God was still watching. The world was for me.

My sister always told me what to wear, where to go, and who to talk to, "because Canada is not Jamaica." Despite this, for most of my life, I thought moving to Canada was the best choice I ever made. I lived at her place for a while, then I moved out, then I moved back at her place, then I finally moved into my own place.

Even though my sister and I didn't get along, I spent a lot of time with her friends who helped me find work. My sister's friends assured me that there was a lot of work and that I would get a job because I was bright. "No problem," they said.

I didn't have money for school, and in my mind, I was saying to myself, "What a wonderful country. I guess I won't be going to school then." It was Cecile's friend Dee Dee who took me around to apply for jobs. The job market at that time was easy once you finished high school;

it was not a problem getting work. I think my beauty and charm went a long way. According to the white Canadian lady at the employment centre, I was not too black, I had a nice smile, I was pretty, she could understand my sentences, I really spoke English well, and I was wearing a lovely dress. I guess youth, brains, and beauty were in my favour.

Within two days of arriving in the big city, I found a job. Dee Dee had taken me to Bell Canada. She told me it was a very good company to work for and was hiring. I remember filling out my first application form, which read Bell Telephone Company of Canada. I wrote in my address on Ontario Street. The next question asked how long I had lived in the city. Two days. What was my education? According to Canadian standards, it was grade twelve, I think. I had a likeable personality and got the job.

I started at the bottom as a clerk five, and my salary rate was sixty-nine Canadian dollars per week, which was the average entry-level pay at the time. The benefits were good, and the work was challenging and enjoyable. I worked with different departments, including construction, accounts payable, and special accounts. I worked with the project manager, assistant manager, and manager and also became a union representative. All of my days at Bell were about hard work and repeatedly proving myself. In July 1973, I was promoted to clerk seven and received a raise, increasing my weekly salary to C$124.25.

Despite my hard work and strong performance, I was as a black woman in a predominantly white company, and racism showed its head numerous times. I always got over it, although one incident was very upsetting, and I will explain. Those who know me well know that I never swear, and I never get mad. I am always a calm, laughable, and prayerful person.

One day I worked for hours straight, decoding numbers and entering data on another sheet to give my boss, Francis, a figure that was needed ASAP. The assignment took me a lot of time, and I felt good informing him it was complete and putting it onto his desk. When the paper went missing from his in basket, I asked around, but no one seemed to know what had happened to it. Frustrated, I asked everyone in front of the boss and demanded to know who took my assignment from his basket. A coworker who had immigrated to Canada from Poland looked at me and said, "You chocolate, I did."

I looked at her, stood up, pushed the desk over, rolled my fist, and was about to punch her when the boss stopped my fist in midair. The desk was rolling over with paper. I was going to knock her brains out. The boss told her to apologize. We looked in the bin. There we saw that she had the rolled up paper. I redid the assignment and moved on—lesson learned.

My confidence and self-esteem helped me to get over the racism that exists; however, my mind was prepared for it. Before I came to Canada, my brother Malcolm had lived in Missouri in the sixties and had explained the mentality of segregation and racism toward blacks. Even though I knew what to expect, it was still upsetting. I can understand the frustration of blacks who experience racial profiling, but the best way to fight it is to have confidence in yourself, great self-esteem, and wonderful, genuine friends who can help you through it. During my time at Bell, I became very well loved by all, both white and black (including the boss), but never the lady who referred to me as chocolate. This tension lasted until I received a promotion and moved out of that department. I stayed at Bell for twenty-seven years and made many friends. One of them was a white Canadian woman, the department vice president, who remains one of my best friends up to this present day.

I received many promotions throughout my time at Bell. Once when promoted at work, I bought a car, moved into a fine apartment, bought the finest clothes, and thought that parties were heaven. I worked during the day at Bell and eventually started working for Eaton's and Sears on evenings and weekends. While working, I also received my business administration diploma from Ryerson Polytechnic Institute. I felt settled in Canada, so I sent for my brother Calvin. Then Calvin sent for Franklyn. My twin brother Dennis stayed home in Jamaica.

During all this time, I partied mostly on Friday and Saturday nights, but I never missed a weekend church service. Everything to me was beauty and fun. There were questions in my mind about whether evil did exist, because everything was so good. There was nothing negative that existed in my life. Weekends were for parties, and the intensity of weekdays was for work and study. Not a problem, man!

I really enjoyed life and made some crazy choices in Canada, living life in the moment. After work, I enjoyed going to Kensington Market, which at the time was known as Jew Town, to get the latest clothes and shoes. My appearance was part of my image and confidence. This is where I would spend my Friday evenings.

I would call my girlfriends and say, "Hey, this is Deloris. Meet me at Bloor and Spadina." They would answer, "Yup! Going shopping?" and I would say, "Yippidy doo!" Then I continued by saying, "I need a new pair of shoes and a designer dress for a wedding on Saturday."

I loved living in the moment and not planning ahead. The ladies thought I was crazy and cutting it very close. The seventies in Toronto was a different time. Friends were very generous. When we went to shop, if I was short, they would pay. If they needed a dress, one of us would buy it. As we showed up in the stores, the owners knew us. After shopping, the night was still young. So, we would go to Yonge Street and check out clubs, including our regular spot—Latin Quarters, which was a Caribbean club. We were usually home by midnight. What great memories. It was the joy of the moment.

One of my fondest memories during this time is my trip to Hawaii with my work colleague. She wanted company on her trip, so I joined her. We travelled for thirteen hours from Toronto to Texas and then to Hawaii. We stayed for ten days and did all of the traditional things, including surfing, going to pig roasts, dancing the Hula to the drum players, and going to the beach. We dressed up every night and looked for the cheapest places to eat. It was awesome.

I visited a few churches but had no interest in them. I went to Presbyterian, Evangelical, Catholic, United, Gospel Hall, Church of God, but I could not be satisfied. I found an excuse for every church. Despite the excitement of my new world, I still had that fear of God, and so I continued to pray. God was still over watching me.

THE TURNING LANE

FROM 1970 TO 1977, life was about studying, having fun, living, enduring a bit of abuse, experiencing disappointments, facing challenges, and learning lessons. I continued to enjoy life to its fullest; I looked forward to weekends when a few girls and I would party, party, party until four o'clock in the morning. We would stroll down Yonge Street and stop at the bar to dance. I recall the La Cock Door and Latin Quarters up a few more stops. That was where most of the mixed race, black, and Caribbean stops were. Everyone went there to dance the night away and maybe catch a date. We chose to be bad, but in a good way. I have never been much of an alcohol drinker. Amazingly, after all that, I would still be in church on Sunday morning by ten.

At that time, men were what were important to me. What a mistake! I remember once being introduced by a friend to this gentleman named Lego. I thought he was a gentleman; he was working and going to school. He had a big Cadillac and money to spend and seemed romantic. The friend said he was a good guy, so I spent time with this good guy for the next two years. One day, and then against the next day, he came to my work to drive me home. He asked, "Why are you working late?"

I said, "It has to do with my job; it's overtime." The next week, he complained there wasn't any food cooked, and he waited for dinner from me.

I was so surprised, and I said, "You do not have a maid. I did not grow up with a father or anyone bossing me around or talking to me like that."

He said, "If I come by tomorrow and you are not there and you did not cook, I will burst your a—!"

I said, "You must be crazy!"

He said, "Try me!" I missed the bus and was late for home. He was there waiting.

When I arrived home, I said, "What's up?" He went inside with me, asked for the food, and gave me a slap in the face. I cried and said, "You are really crazy!" I broke off the relationship.

Then he said, "No one will ever get you. I will throw acid in your face before I let you leave!"

I told my girlfriends what had happened, and they were all upset and protected me. I still always lived alone, although I was sharing an apartment with a roommate across from me.

Within a few weeks, he came back and asked for forgiveness and bought me a car. I was so happy. I thought he was okay and would not do it again. He took me out of my apartment and put me into his apartment. Then I had more time to spend with him, and it stated to get bad again. The evenings were like hell. I did not want to go home. The fighting always started with him asking me questions: Why were you late? Who called? Who drove you home? Why is the food not ready? Why did you cook rice and not dumplings? The list went on every day and so did the abuse. I was scared, but I was so fed up. With the way I was brought up and with my confidence and self-esteem, I wasn`t going to take it anymore. I moved out when he left for work one day. I pretended I was going to work, but then I went out, came back in, and packed my suitcase. I left everything else behind.

I thought it was done, but I was wrong. That was just the beginning of hell. He stalked me for another two years and tried to punch me out on many occasions. He would usually wait for me in an underground garage or at the bus stop. Eventually, I had to get a restraining order to keep him away from my home and workplace. I must give credit to Canadian legal system, which helped me a lot at that time. After I got that devil out of my life through legal action, I felt as free as a bird outside of a cage. I never had abuse in my life growing up, so it still puzzles me why I attracted it. It has never left my mind. I now think of it as a lesson or journey that some of us need to go through. Now that I am a counsellor, this experience helps me to relate to others who are in abusive situations. No one should ever stay in an abusive situation, and help is out there for victims. As someone who went through the experience, trust me when I say that it is worth it to leave, no matter how bad things are. Then life goes on—the next chapter of life.

My life moved on, but heaven kept crashing down on me when life met me at a crossroads, and I fell ill. I kept fainting without explanation. I would pass out at work during the week and every Saturday night. I'd wake up not knowing what day it was only to find out I had been in a trance for up to two days. I went to the hospital every Saturday night, and each time the doctors would tell me that nothing was wrong. One day, someone I knew from back home in Jamaica said to me, "Deloris, you are not the person I knew anymore." After sharing my story about what was happening, she said, "You need spiritual help." Seeking solace, I took my holidays and did everything possible to find my way out of my illness. Unfortunately, at the same time, God started talking to me. In a short time I lost my car, my apartment, the man in my life, and even some of my friends. God took it all away and called me.

In calling me, God worked through a girlfriend who introduced me to a minister who advised me that in order for me to receive healing, I would have to ask for forgiveness and start doing the work of God. She told me I would have to attend a special type of church, the ones that wrap their heads—Zionist, Spiritual Baptist, or Evangelical Baptist.

At this point, I was too proud. No way! I didn't even understand what she was talking about. It so happened that when I was saying "no way," God was saying "you'd better." My fainting spells were replaced by something more puzzling. I would go off into spiritual trances, dancing, chanting, and repeating spiritual messages. This would happen most often on Saturday nights or when I heard drums or music at parties. When I revived, I quickly found myself answering like Jonah, Isaiah, and Jeremiah, saying, "Here am I. Send me." I had long thought that I was too sinful to do His work. It was only when I looked around and saw the fountain of living water that I remembered my beautiful childhood days. The Bible had opened up before me. In these moments, I made a covenant to God, but it wouldn't last. I kept going to parties and living my life as I had before.

Although I still partied, I had heard what my Lord wanted me to do. I wanted to begin working for Him, so I found a small Spiritual Baptist Zionist Church and worked with a beautiful lady for a few years. One day during a church trip to New York, I met a lady who shared a spiritual insight with me. She said, "Young lady. Girl, you have a gift to teach and preach the word of God! You are a born healer! You must go to a special type of church!" I rejected her message and thought these women were crazy. I pitied her and wished never to see her again.

Back in Toronto, I was a party one night in 1970. I was on the dance floor and heard the song "Oh! Africa!" playing. While dancing, I fell into a trance on the floor and passed out. I woke up at Toronto East General Hospital around midnight. These episodes continued again for a few months, so I decided to go only to private parties. The same thing started happening at work, and I would fall down under my desk. It happened all the time. My girlfriend from the states, who is still a true friend, said to me one day, "Deloris, you need to see somebody spiritual." Then she laughed very hard and added, "Girl, you are going crazy!"

I took her seriously and thought about the medical doctors who said nothing was wrong with me. So, I travelled to New York again, but to my disappointment, it was just to hear that I needed to do spiritual work, follow the Lord, live the life of a saint, and wrap my head. This seemed absurd and unpleasant to me. Once again I dismissed all these sayings.

Returning home to Toronto, I had only a room that I rented for sixty-nine Canadian dollars a month, a small radio, and no TV. I only had ten Canadian dollars in the bank and didn't have any credit cards. One night I went to work at Eaton's in the returns department and met two sisters I knew from the club Abida and Afrida. They were from Trinidad and Tobago. They helped me out with bus fare and gave me some dhal and roti to eat. I was grateful. They told me about the people in Trinidad and Tobago who wrapped their heads. I asked, "Are they like the ones in Jamaica? If so, I do not think that those are Christians." I laughed, because never understood those movements and had no idea what they were all about.

One day I fainted again at work, but this time when I woke up, I remember what the lady in New York told me and went straight down to Eaton's, got myself an Eaton's credit card, and bought two yards of blue and red cloth. I said the prayer "The Lord is my Shepherd," which I remembered from when I was a child, and wrapped my head in the store. As soon as I wrapped it, I felt better. I kept it on during my lunch but removed it before going back to work and hid my head wrap in my purse. After work, I put it on in the car.

Years went by with laughter and fun, but I continued to have trances. I could not control myself, so I continued to wrap my head occasionally. I realised it was getting worse, however, because I began seeing and hearing things and other people's business. Taking more advice from the spiritual mothers, I went searching for churches. Finally, I met a woman named Mommy Brickley with a church at Woodbine and Kingston. When I went in to see her, she was in the middle of prayer meeting. She welcomed me and gave me a psalm to read. I did so and went back the next week. I continued worshiping in Mommy Brickley's basement.

I dressed in my suit with my briefcase on weekdays, and during evenings and weekends, I'd put on my long skirt, wrap my head, and help with healing in the basement for sick people, doing things I did not understand. I was so naive and just went along with everything. I tried to hide from everyone that I was worshiping in a basement and wrapping my head, but my sister in Canada phoned home to Jamaica and told everyone that I was going mad.

The whole idea of this movement—the head-wrap movement and spiritual information—seemed mystical. All I knew about was the Anglican Church, Church of God, and Catholics. My personal experiences were real. However, I was still on a quest to understand my inner self. I eventually rented a room at Mommy's house. There I got my healing, my nurturing, and my spiritual training.

FAMILY LIFE

As I continued my journey as a young, black, beautiful woman, I must admit my soul cried out for true love and genuine people in my life. I was looking for people who cared not for my outer but my inner beauty. I was on a quest for companions with like minds and I was deeply spiritual, so I went to retreats, did meditation, and prayed every day as if I were the priest in the church. These few months I went around visiting churches, so I could experience different religions and variations of spiritual diversity. Mostly I would go from church to church because I did not want to get stuck heading any church activities. As soon as a pastor wanted me to teach Sunday school, join the choir, do next week's lesson, or attend a convention, I would take off to another church the next week.

I was amazed to see the huge churches, with mostly white Canadians who attended. It was a deep contrast to the type of churches I grew up going to. However, their devotion, songs, and meditations were the same. It was similar, so I was able to embrace the culture. At times like this, I realised that no matter how different people are or how they grow up, we are all spiritual beings and very similarly on a quest for the same mission. During my moments of church hopping, I met lots of wonderful praying people who encouraged me on my spiritual journey.

One summer evening a girlfriend invited me to a spiritualist church at Lansdowne and Ossington where they gave messages through the mediumship of the dead. When I entered the church, there was no greeter; it was almost as if they assumed you knew where to go and what you were getting into. I didn't. I entered from the main hallway and sat down among the small congregation of about twenty people. Everyone was quietly waiting for the service to start. Three people in semiformal attire walked onto the altar from the basement. A lady approached the podium and introduced the three people. There was one black minister named Vernon Batson and two white female ministers. They were healers and spiritual mediums. Throughout the service, they would get up one at a time and speak in funny voices to the congregation about what will and will not happen and what they should look for. The black minister spoke the most, addressing a particular person in the congregation.

"You, lady in the red hat," he said. "I have a message for you from Tom, your uncle, who passed away two years ago."

"Yes," responded the lady in red. "My uncle Tom passed away." With that confirmation, he began telling the details of the spiritual message from her ancestors.

I was very curious. In my mind, I told myself I would be back, although it was a bit scary. The service was completed in about an hour, after which the mediums all came down to greet everybody. Reverend Batson did not speak to me directly during service, but afterward he approached me. He was shorter than me, and at least ten years older. Speaking with a strong English accent, he looked directly at me and said, "I will see you again."

I just shrugged and answered, "I dunno." Shortly afterward, my friend and I left.

That Monday night I received a call from the reverend. I had left my name and number in the visitors' book, and he was calling to follow up on the night before. The conversation was brief, and he invited me to another place near Coxwell where he served as a minister. It was a Spiritual Baptist Church in his basement. I hadn't been to a Spiritual Baptist Church yet, so I agreed to go. When I didn't show up to the church later that week, he called again several times. Each time our conversations got a little longer. He kept calling. He called and called and called, and we kept talking. Finally, I decided I would take him up on his offer and go to the church in his basement.

That Saturday night, as I approached the house, I went down a short, lit staircase into the basement. As I entered the door, I saw everyone's shoes, so I removed mine as well. The main room was set up just like churches I had seen before. There were candles at the entrance, and the four corners were lit up with candlelight. A faint aroma of incense enveloped the room, which was filled with different statues of saints. In the middle of the floor was a circle of lights, which I later learned was called the centre pole. As my eyes reached up toward the front, I saw the high altar full of beautiful flowers, more candlelight, a glass pitcher of water, and a picture of the cross.

The service reminded me of my time at Mommy Brickley's. I felt completely at home. The psalms were read, and there was lots of chanting and singing with drums. With the beating of the drums, I fell under the influence on the spirit, and all I could recall was ending up on the floor. I noticed that most of the church members had disappeared. For the first time, I was afraid. What happened to me? What took place? The pastor assured me that there was nothing to be afraid of.

After service, I went home and spoke to my spiritual mother. She said, "You will leave me and soon marry him. You will have children. However, never ask him about his previous life." And then she laughed. Her words surprised me. Not about his previous life as a medium, because I knew he'd had many past lives. He believed in reincarnation. I was surprised about the rest of it, but she was right.

We kept in touch, and he continued calling me. He was fascinated by my youth and spirituality. Once he invited me out, but I was on my way out to visit my parents in Jamaica. So, he offered to take me to the airport instead, and he did. When I came back, he called every night, and that was when I realised he was really interested in me. I was interested in him too. He was caring, very spiritual, and extremely hard working; had a great prophetic voice; and was a bishop. He was truly a romantic man; he really loved me. I dreamt about him, even the books he was reading I dreamt. We got married in April 1977, seven months after we met.

Throughout our courtship, I noticed a growing hostility among some members of the church. Some of the older women would make comments: "Where did this woman come from?" "She is too young for him." "Oh, she's a Jamaican."

When the wedding invitations went out, there was an even a greater commotion. Close friends denied and persecuted me because of my relationship with Vernon and the church. Some even walked away like Judas. The older women in the church took all of their belongings from the church, including their robes, tambourines, shakers, and even their slippers. "You can keep the young girl," they told him. "We are gone! We are disappointed that you are not staying single. You will have no more time for us."

Their loss was my gain. God had provided me with a husband, a home, a family, and a church. As His word says, "These I have added unto you because you obeyed me" Matthew 6:33. We were well cared for and had a great home full of good laughter and good food. Vernon was a great cook. His sweet bread was the best. My husband was the main cook, because that was his profession before ministry. He had a voice to sing, knew how to read music, and could carry a good note for all the songs. I recognized that I had been spoiled by my dad, but Vernon spoiled me even more. Our life together lasted eleven years—1977 to 1982 were the golden years of marriage and children. We had two sons, and our family life revolved around the church. I was the happiest first lady in town with a marriage so great that it must have been made in heaven. There would be no parting until death. Rest in peace, Vernon.

My husband cared deeply for his children. My first pregnancy was easy, and I remained very active, participating in all church activities, such as mourning and baptisms. The sisters were concerned that I was doing too much. On the day my first son, Jezreel, was born, it was icy outside. I remember the car skidding down the Don Valley Parkway as my husband rushed me to the hospital. He was born within the hour. I named him Jezreel, because at his birth I heard a voice telling me that he was a boy and I should name him Jezreel. My husband agreed, as he has always trusted my instincts.

I came later to learn by looking through the Bible that his name means "to sow" and is a valley in Africa. Jezreel was christened at St. Paul Anglican Church where his godmother attended, because our church did not have all the credentials yet. I had my Anglican confirmation certificate from Jamaica, so it was no problem. I had only six months off of work to stay home and then went back to a better position.

Five years later, I was pregnant again. My second pregnancy was not as easy. I was ordered to stay off my feet and stayed home from work for three months before Josiah was born. My husband was working at church and missed the delivery. Our two sons were very good growing up. They listened and sat still all through church. Once I had to drop them off at the doctor's office and run an errand. When I got back, the doctor was amazed at how well my two "gentlemen" had behaved. I told him it was genetic; he laughed and said, "Good for you."

Life revolved around the church. I had a passion for church and loved church work, so I continued to work closely with my husband to build the church. Our organization was one of the first establishments in the 1970s.

Every time someone writes or misquotes the Spiritual Baptist's original foundation in Toronto Canada, I have to correct them. The truth is this: There were four Spiritual Churches in Toronto in 1973, and two were known as Spiritual Baptists. One of those two was one of the first founded Spiritual Baptist Churches known as St. Frederic's, which was incorporated in 1976. The two cofounders were the late Bishop Vernon Batson and I, Deloris Seiveright. There came other spiritual leaders with groups, but I am not sure when they became established or incorporated in Toronto.

My husband and I were engaged in our spiritual lives and performed mournings and fastings and were involved in many church trips. Our missions took us to Trinidad and Tobago to meet with the official founders of the Spiritual Baptists. I got off the plane, and there were the bishop, other mothers, and my spiritual mother. They always used two cars to come for me, because so many people wanted to greet me at the airport. If they had taken one car, they would have had to either take me and leave the suitcase or take the suitcase and leave me. When I came out of customs, they would all be there, hugging and greeting and asking about the flight. When we got into the car, everyone wanted to sit beside me. Finally, we were on our way to Port of Spain or Laventille or Marval or the place where I would be staying.

On our way, we stopped to get coconut water, my favourite drink. I was well looked after. They would always ask me what I wanted for breakfast, lunch, and dinner. They cooked and washed my clothes, and someone would take me into the town, either by Maxi Taxi or car. They never left me alone; they always had to shop around me, hold my bag, take me to the car, and follow behind or beside me on the busy streets. No one could touch me. I was an honoured minister and archbishop in Trinidad and Tobago. I was their queen. On whatever occasion I went to Trinidad for, whether it was a liberation celebration, ordination, or mourning, the trip was always amazing and fulfilling.

During my trip, I took a leap of faith and went to mourn (fast) with then Mother Superior Elaine Griffiths, wife and official cofounder of the Spiritual Baptist Faith around the world. I stayed there in Trinidad fasting for seven days and then rested for three more days before flying back to Toronto. The vision became very clear that part of my spiritual development involved a swift growth through the hierarchies. Mother Superior, in turn, connected with our organization here in Canada. Following this visit, Vernon my husband and I spent most of our money incorporating the church and travelling to Trinidad twice a year. We also invited and hosted ministers from there who came and enjoyed our establishment in Toronto.

We had helpers in my home, mostly from Trinidad and Tobago, who were familiar with the religion and helped me understand the religion as I raised my children. Many people think that I was born in Trinidad or went to school there, because of my affiliations. Trinidad has become like my second home that I visit regularly. My mentors encourage me to teach wherever I go. Whenever I have been in Trinidad during the past thirty-five years, I have preached and met the media, the government, and the Spiritual Baptist community. My first son is now thirty-two, and I have been teaching, mourning, and going to Trinidad since before my two sons were born. Trinidad and Tobago travel experiences always have me thinking about the good old days.

Life was good for a while, but I remember the moment my life took another turn. Like all humans, Vernon had a weakness and a past. He had friends from a wilder past, a very different life from the one I knew him to lead. As the years went by, he had learned to grow apart from his old friends. One time, however, some of his old acquaintances from England who knew his past came to visit. During their three-month visit, I learned things I wish I hadn't heard. I didn't know right away. In fact, I was the last one to know or recognize anything. I was too focused on the church and the children. During those months, I often recalled the words of my Spiritual Mother: "Never ask him about his previous life."

At first, I didn't believe them and was in denial. In fact, sometimes I still don't believe them. I defended him for a year against all accusations until I came home that Sunday evening and asked Vernon if he'd had a part in any of these things. His replied, "That was the past." Although he said the words, he was not able to forgive himself. He hid his past to protect his wife and children, and now that he had been exposed, he was unable to cope.

During this time of challenges and new things, we went to quite a few counselling sessions, but if one of the parties has set in his mind it cannot work out, it will never be mended. He moved from our master bedroom and stayed in the guestroom for two years. Jezreel, our oldest son, was angry and hurt and never spoke to Vernon, although I begged him to. Josiah was much younger at the time and remained very close to Vernon and spoke to him at all times. In 1989, we bought separate homes but were very civil. Each of our homes was where we nurtured our children and balanced our lives, but we spoke to each other every week and would share stories about our sons, their schoolwork, and their relationship and visits with him.

Raising two sons alone was challenging at times. My eldest son stayed close to me and participated in church and was involved with church activities. One day his teacher called and wanted to see me. He was so frightened. His teacher wanted to let me know how impressed she was with his work. He had written about the role models in his life, and I had been one of them. I went through a rough time keeping my second son in secondary school. Many days he did not want to go, and if he did go, he would stay in the cafeteria. I received a lot of help from the school counsellors and all the prayer warriors at church. On Father's Day, I always received a card from him, because he said that I was a mother and father in one.

As a single mother who worked, was in school, and was active in church, life continued nonstop. I knew that I needed to reignite myself. I booked a flight from work, went home, packed, and left the next morning. I asked the helper, friends, and Vern to watch over the children. He thought I was crazy, but he knew I needed the break. I took two weeks and went to Colombia, a Spanish-speaking country run by an army. I checked into a hotel and knew no one there. I made friends with the front desk clerks; the girls showed me around, took me to their local homes, and came to my room to get spiritual advice when they found out who I was. I even met people from Toronto who were on cruises.

One day I decided to take a walk all by myself through town and sat on a bench. A man approached me, sat down beside me, and said, "You should go back to your hotel; it is not safe to walk around alone."

When I looked down at his ankle, there was a gun strapped to it. Apparently, he was a police officer. I took off to my room quickly. Thanks be to God!

One September night back in Toronto, as I was finishing some last-minute packing for a flight to England that left in less than five hours, the doorbell rang. It was 10:30 at night. Jezreel was on vacation in Jamaica, and Josiah, who was seventeen, was upstairs in his room. I asked myself, "Who could that be at this time?" I looked out and saw three people at the door.

One voice rang out. "It's me."

"Me who?" I asked. It was Vern's sister and two ministers from the church. "What happened?" I asked as I opened the door.

Vern's sister immediately asked for Josiah, but I told her he was in bed. "Tell me what it is," I insisted. "He's sleeping."

"His dad passed away last night," she said.

When? Where? How? They provided me with no details, except for the fact that Vernon had passed during a trip to the United States. The year was 1999. I sat down and told them to come in and bawled my eyes out for a good fifteen minutes. Josiah heard me crying and came down. He saw us and asked what had happened. We told him, and all of us continued bawling into the night. The ministers and Vern's sister sympathized with me. They informed me that by the time the body would arrive from the states and the arrangements were made, Jezreel and I would be back from our trips for the viewing and funeral. At that time, I felt going away was the best thing for me. I wanted to be alone with my thoughts and memories of him, so I left to catch my flight.

In England, I had a headache for the first two days. The lady I stayed with in London and friends from Trinidad who were there brought me great comfort. I went to see a spiritual counsellor for guidance, who told me to just relax and that my sons would be okay. I phoned home every night to check on them. My sister visited Josiah and Jezreel throughout the week to support and comfort them while I was away.

When I came back from England, Josiah told me that some of his dad's associates had come by the house. Josiah didn't understand much at the time, so when they went to Vern's house and claimed they were collecting the fridge, sweaters, and many other items they had lent Vern over the years, Josiah in his grief did not stop them. They had keys, and he left them in the house. They took all the things they wanted. I had to get a lawyer to tell the kids their rights and to put a stop to people coming in and out of the house. The house needed cleaning, so I had to clean it. I cleaned that house on my hands and knees, got rid of all the junk, and called a real estate agent friend to put the house up for sale. The house was just part of it. In death, things always become complicated.

The church that the bishop and I had founded together was going downhill. Although I had not been involved for more than ten years, church members called me with their concerns. Many felt that some of those in charge were confused. Everyone wanted to be a leader and the boss. It is important that organizations, churches, and families prepare succession plans. We never plan the day or the hour when anyone goes, and it's always a very emotional time when loss happens, especially when it is unexpected. It was a difficult time, but our family and the church family got through it.

In my journey in life there are people who come in and out. Some are sent to do specific work and move one. Some come because I chose to let them in. However, as soon as some people get toxic, my spirit uses the antitoxins and flushes them out. This is how I survive negative vibrations. I must admit, there are some people I miss very much, but as the saying goes, we must let go and move on.

Vernon will always be remembered as a stalwart leader. May his soul forever rest in peace.

Nurturing a Gift

" "THEY THAT WAIT upon the Lord shall renew their strength and mount up with wing like an eagle, they shall run and not be weary walk and not faint. Teach me Lord to wait." (Isa. 40:31)

I am always wearing a lot of hats. At times, it was challenging raising two boys, running a ministry, working full-time, and attending classes. I don't think about the toll of everything most of the time. However, one cold night when I was about forty-eight years old, I prayed for a change. I had my studies in business administration and was struggling with what else to do. As a leading member of the church, I attended occasional Bible classes. One day I visited a class and received a message that I should go to college. I thought it would be to my benefit, because I loved quoting the scripture, to take a few courses. The question was, what should I study?

I had some interest in completing my CGA (Certified General Accounting) degree. Working in the finance department at Bell, I had already completed some of the courses, and I loved working with numbers. However, I also loved words and speaking with people while serving at the church, preaching, and teaching Sunday school. I realised that if I was going to speak or preach, and because I liked to do everything so perfect, I should know the Bible and theology well. Therefore, I decided to move ahead with my plans. I called up Tyndale, a Bible college in Ontario where I studied for eight years.

I registered at the student registrar's office for preaching class. I was accepted at the office to be in the class; however, when I arrived on the first day, the teacher looked at me and said, "Are you sure you are in the right class?"

"Yes," I replied. "Isn't this the preaching class?"

He said, "Yes. Are you aware that it is only men who take the preaching class?"

I said, "I was not aware of this. I was accepted at the office, and although I am a woman, I want to take this class."

He hesitated and said, "You are sure the office knows this is the class you should be in?"

In turn, I said to him, "Is my name on the list for the class?" He confirmed, and I said, "Well, then I am in this class. It is up to you to check with the registration office, but I am in this class."

The class began, and the next week I went back. The teacher told me he had checked with the registrar, and all was okay. As the class continued, it came time for preaching practice, and everyone had dates to preach a fifteen-minute sermon on special subjects. Each person would grade one another, and the teacher would also grade and then give a final grade. This special night, it was my turn to preach. I preached from the Old Testament, Haggai 1, which relates to building God's house. I preached for fifteen minutes, and you could have heard a pin drop in the place. It was dead silence except for my voice. For the next fifteen minutes, they all evaluated me. The evaluation from everyone was A minus. The teacher asked me if I had preached before and if I preached now. I hesitated to answer. I smiled, because I didn't want to let him know that I was an experienced preacher. This was just for the paper.

After class, the teacher said to me, "You deserve an A plus, but I will give you an A minus."

Class was over, and we all went outside. I went to my car, and two of the men came to my car. "You have blessed me tonight with your words," one of them said to me. "If you have not been preaching, start preaching, and if you are preaching, keep preaching. You are gifted. I apologize we could not have said this in the class."

I had to deal with the challenges and experiences that stemmed from the bias that woman should not take the position of a pastor, as held by some of my colleagues. Despite this, I had great teachers who saw my potential and realised that I had Great Spirit within me.

So many people have experienced what I had just experienced. Some would have quit, and others would have changed their courses. My advice to those who read my story is to never give up or quit the things that you are gifted in and have passion for, because you will never be able to help the way you should help. Schooling at a mature age was fun, not hard, and very spiritual, because I understood the calling of God's work. I graduated with a major in pastoral and a minor in counselling.

When you are gifted at something and it is meant to happen, doors will open. When I arrived in Canada, studying pastoral ministry was far from my mind, although I had eaten and breathed church while growing up. These activities have become a natural part of my life. I would feel sick or guilty if I did not go to church or read my Bible. A significant part of my life was facing my calling as a minister and how my life unfolded smoothly into the very career that that I avoided when I was seventeen.

While serving with Vernon, I started out as Sister Del, progressed to Mother Del, then Mother Leader, then Reverend Mother, then Right Reverend Mother Superior. I can say that it was not of my own doing, but the Christ that lived in me. He had placed me in ministry and used me to proclaim His word. In my personal life, I have gained strength from the Creator, according to Psalm 121:1-2: "My help cometh from the Lord which makes heaven and earth." The moment I made a career transition,

I realised the crossroads I met were made to strengthen my path. As I ventured into ministry, I realised my life was not mine but the Lord's, and people would demand and ask for expertise (my gift). However, I know when to care for myself. Self-care is the greatest thing one can attain. Self-care lets you think about yourself as you think about others.

In 1996, as with all businesses, Bell Canada decided to restructure. They were handing out severance packages, and this was the perfect opportunity for me to fully engage myself into my passion for ministry. I took the package and went into ministry full time on June 26, 1996. I still had my childlike humility with me and lots of energy. Praise be to God! He had brought me thus far, but I knew there were more crossroads to meet. My friends and family threw me a great retirement party. There were so many touching words shared. It was a surprise to me that Dennis, my twin, was coming up. Everything was kept from me.

The planning for my party was done by my past supervisors. They got all the clippings of my childhood from my son and my daughter in-law. They got everything they could have gotten hold of. A great team of men and women had out done themselves. It was an evening of laughter, dancing, and a lot of stories. They loved to call me Mrs. Batson, because I'd told people at work that no one from my birthplace addressed any boss or peers by their first names, but they still called me Deloris. That is the Canadian way. I danced my new shoes off. I still own those expensive shoes today, the ones that I bought on Yonge Street just for my retirement ball at Bell Canada. All the managers and the vice presidents came to my party. They really loved me. I really worked hard.

Retirement came in 1996, but my life was just beginning. Less than two weeks after retirement, reality sets in. I realised I would be getting a smaller paycheque and would have to find another career. The company paid us for three months to change careers through a career transition agency. It was fun, but I knew I had to continue with the religious ministry.

One day a few years later I looked up on my roof and around the house and realised the house needed to be repainted, the windows needed to be replaced, and the roof needed to be redone, but there wasn't any money to do everything. However, with faith and perseverance, I was able to get everything done with the help of a big line of credit as I remortgaged my house yet again.

I opened up a counselling company and a website later. However, I did a lot of work in counselling from the heart as a volunteer. I could not live only on this. I ventured into the ministry full time in helping youths. As the passage says, "Promotion cometh neither from the east nor from the south, but God is the single judge. He putteth down one and setteth up another" (Ps. 75:6-7). Alleluia.

SPIRITUAL BAPTIST—
HUMBLE BEGINNINGS

"Make a joyful noise unto the Lord, all ye lands." (Ps. 100:1)

WE CELEBRATE ACCORDING to Psalm 100, "making a joyful noise" by the chants of spiritual songs, trumpets, and prayers, which led us to freedom. It can be said that the slave who came from Africa brought his or her heritage with them to the Caribbean. Despite attempts by white Europeans to break Africans' connections with their homeland through severe oppression and religious indoctrination, the African spirit persevered. This is evident even in modern-day Caribbean and black North American culture. The European Christianity and Africans' faith emerge as Shouters Spiritual Baptists, embracing the chanting, robes, head wraps, drumming, and other elements of Africanism. Shouters Spiritual Baptist is a Christian faith with biblical language used in the worship and all the spiritual rituals. The beliefs and practices are rich, meaningful, and powerful. The Shouters believe in the omnipresent, omniscient, and omnipotent—the qualities of the Father, Son, and Holy Spirit as expressed by Him, God, the Creator that sustains the universe. God is both known and unknown, and the Holy Spirit is the comforter and instructor.

The Shouters Spiritual Baptist faith was officially established in Trinidad and Tobago, although it is sometimes debated that Shouters also existed in St. Vincent and other regions of the Caribbean, which is true. However, there is no debate that Trinidad and Tobago was the island that took the lead to appeal the oppression of the faith that was legislated through The Shouters Prohibition Ordinance. According to the Shouter Prohibition Ordinance, 1917, "It shall be an offence for any person to hold or take part in or to attend any Shouters' meeting or for any Shouters' meeting to be held in any part of the Colony indoors or in the open air at any time of the day or night."

The Ordinance, in effect, drove the Shouters underground for the next three decades until it was repealed in Parliament on March 30, 1951. Credit for getting the ban lifted goes to elders of the faith, led by the late Supreme Archbishop Elton George Griffith, who, in October 1949, delivered a petition to then Governor Sir John Shaw. In response, the governor appointed a committee to investigate the Shouters. Almost a year after the report, the committee voted unanimously in favour of repealing the Ordinance, and this paved the way for the removal of the stigma attached to the Shouters. When the bill was passed in Parliament at noon on March 30, 1951, Pastor Deacon Griffith was carried by his followers into Woodford Square in Trinidad and Tobago where there was a great rejoicing among the hundreds of Shouters and their well-wishers. In Toronto, the spiritual Baptist Faith came to Toronto by migration of Trinidadians and people from all over the Caribbean.

The Shouters faith has its own traditions that have been practiced all over the world before, during, and after the time of oppression, up to now. Looking across the congregation, one can see women with their heads tied in white or multicoloured cloths. Men, women, and children all sit together and wear robes that are similar to clergy but are African—or Indian-inspired—colourful, ornate, and very cultural. As the service proceeds, there will be shouting, chanting, and shaking. According to the working of the Spirit, the use of perfume, incense, or chalk for sealing may be used.

The Shouter Baptist always start worship service with hymns from old traditions, such as the Anglican, Methodist, and Catholic song books, the congregation sings to the beating of the drums: "When I survey the wondrous cross on which the Prince of Glory died; my richest gain I count but loss, and pour contempt on all my pride."

As the hymn continues, the mothers of the church slowly proceed to the corners of the room to begin surveying the space using the oil, water, and sweet perfume while ringing the Bell to bring in the spirit. The Bells continue to ring at different intervals throughout the service. These rituals consecrate the space as the temple for worship. We pray with a Lota and Taria (religious vessels) and flowers. Here we are to start our worship session. Archbishop, bishops, and ministers go into prayers at the altar, followed by the mothers' prayers at the centre pole, a pole with twelve flags representing the tribes of Israel mentioned throughout the Bible in Genesis, Numbers, Chronicles, and Revelation.

There are seven lit candlesticks, which represent the seven churches in Revelation 2:1, and a glass of water with white flowers, milk, and sweet perfume for the spirit of worship or healing. The archbishop or ministers take the floor and either start reading from the Psalms or Gospels or immediately start with their message for the main sermon. After the preaching, there is anointing or laying on of hands, depending on the manifestation of the spirit. We shout and chant. There is a lot of drumming, chanting, and praising God. Sometimes our bodies and limbs shake along with the vibration. This part of the service is no different from other Pentecostal worship, just more groaning and loud tongues, hard shaking of the body, manifestation of prophesy, and dancing in the spirit of rejoicing.

For new believers wishing to practice, washing and anointing is the first step into the faith, followed by baptism by immersion in a river, lake, or sea. Other traditions include thanksgiving, or feeding the people, which can take place at church or at any household. This blessing, along with offerings and tithes, are offered by all Shouter Baptists monthly, yearly, or as the spirit bids. Another important part of our faith is Spiritual retreat, also known as mourning. This period of retreat consists of praying, partial or complete fasting, meditating, singing of praise, and thanksgiving over a period of seven to forty days. Most commonly, it is seven days. Attending a Shouter service is a great experience and one of the best things anyone can ever do.

The church is now officially known as The National Evangelical Spiritual Baptist Faith and has been registered in Trinidad and Tobago since 1945 and now in Toronto since 1974 under the leadership of myself, Archbishop Dr. Deloris Seiveright Founder. In 1988 in Trinidad, I was consecrated as bishop, founder, and overseer of the Shouters National Evangelical Spiritual Baptist Faith (N.E.S.B.F) in Toronto. My spiritual parents, Archbishop Elton and Mother Superior Elaine, saw within me my spiritual goals and values and continued to show me the ways to carry out ceremonies of all kinds.

As a woman in my new position, challenges faced me in several ways. Women were not allowed to be leaders, pastors, or bishops, according most religions. It so happened that I was the unruly one. Many men resented the idea of a women being a bishop. Lessons came along the way, but I learned very fast. I learned to ignore distracting things. For instance, I learned to ignore people who asked, "Why is that woman Deloris moving so fast? How is she doing this? What is her secret?" I chose not to let this get the better of me. I exemplified the strength of woman and had a voice ordained by God to be heard. I could not help myself. I had to listen to God's call of healing, teaching, and preaching.

I had had a vision. It was of a place where I was healing people from all over. There were many faces, and it was a Sunday morning. I figured that most people will grow to respect the pledge that I have taken to follow the Lord and let Him guide my footsteps with His infinite, divine light and the Holy Spirit.

In 1989, Shouters National Evangelical Spiritual Baptist Faith International Centre of Canada in Toronto received its incorporation form the Government of Canada. The vision was unfolding. Shouters had a home in the west end. It was in the basement of a shop owned by a wonderful woman named Cindy. It was a small group of us—me, my two sons, the helper Bernadette, and Sis Joyce, a church sister who devoted her time to my family and the church. God Bless her always. It felt like heaven, and we worshipped with high praise. Sometimes there were only six of us and sometimes more.

I remember that the first person to pray at Shouters was Bishop Batson. He, Mother Elaine Griffiths, and another Bishop from Trinidad and Tobago were a part of the consecration. The word had gotten out when we had our official opening on August 28, 1989. It was published in the *Share* newspaper. There were so many people who attended, and everyone was being healed and delivered. What was once as small as a prayer group had grown into a medium-sized church. Yes, we did it all—we ordained, we baptized, we anointed. We also grew out of that basement temple of ours.

Cindy was pleased when we found a wonderful place on Kennedy Road in Scarborough. Just over a decade later, I went to Montreal and met Mother F and Leader C. We spoke and went to the lawyer at Sherbrooke near St. Catherine's to incorporate Rose of Sharon and sign documents. I went over to see some friends at Chambly, had lunch, and then returned to La Salle where I had Sunday service. It was a great event with nice, very warm people. We had an outdoor barbeque after the service and then travelled back on the plane.

I guess it was predestined that I would be the head of a religion that I had no knowledge of in Jamaica or when I arrived in Canada. I have been the archbishop of the Shouters in Canada since 1996 with an honorary doctorate in Sacred Theology from St. Andrew Theological Seminary in London, England. I had to learn the rituals quickly in order to help all members and those who are called in the faith. I am dedicated my cause to study and have mourned more than ten times. I have strongly developed my mind, body, and soul for this vocation.

I do enjoy my spirituality and am proud of a faith that I can attest to as being awesome and meaning a lot to me. Now I live and breathe Spiritual Baptist. I am humble to be in a faith that most people take for granted. It is one indigenous to the Caribbean and rich with the elements of the African Diaspora. Due to the history of slavery in Toronto, very few speak openly about the faith, like all the Caribbean islands. It is as if it were still banned to practice the religion. The Shouters Spiritual Baptist movement was surpassed by worshipping from 1917 to 1951; it is also surpassed by those who do not understand the dynamics of the faith, the dogma that follows the faith.

In order to teach about the Spiritual Baptist Faith in Canada and anyone I try to release the negative and embrace the positive to show them that the faith is great. So it has been placed on my heart to work on increasing the awareness of the faith and let us, the Spiritual Baptists, be known in Canada. Faith is awesome, unique, powerful, mystical, and precious. It is no different from the background I came from (Pentecostal, Anglican, and a touch of Catholic). I am a prophetess, a psychic, a reader, a healer, and an anointed one—a person who has a prophetic voice. I use meditation, the mystical energy, vibration, healing, and the power of the inner mind, soul, and body for the walks of my spiritual lives. I can name them all, but the experience is phenomenal. In the book *Nation Dance* (page 21), I call the faith "a diamond." I am very proud, yet humble to be the cofounder of such a great faith in Toronto.

I have regarded the mercies of God and His blessings as acts of divine favour or compassion. His has extended His kindness to me. God's understanding surpasses that of human minds. He knows our failures and shortcomings, our sins, our infirmities, and our needs. I know for sure that I have approached God, and I have accessed His mercy. He has blessed me, and I'm doubly blessed when I show mercy to others.

The Spiritual Baptist Faith grew in Toronto as my membership grew. We had open-air meetings, press releases, and involvement from partners and other Non-Governmental Organization (NGOs). The baptism ritual in Toronto is great to see. We baptize in the name of the Father, Son, and Holy Ghost as John the Baptist, the forerunner of Jesus, did. We tarry all night, praying, chanting, and calling the adoption, which means the groaning in the Spirit. Before the baptism, we believe in a cleansing bath of herbs, which, according to the scripture, is a healing to the nation. As the night goes on, we then pray and depart to the water/lake before the rising of the sun. The water is cold, but the hearts of the baptizers and candidates are hot of spiritual knowledge and wisdom. The faith carries an awesome manifestation inwardly and outwardly. Everywhere I go, the faith engulfs my being. Everybody knows that I am a Spiritual Baptist. I kept the faith as a Shouter, and I am a Shouter Spiritual Baptist.

The Baptist hymns are from the old hymns and trumpets or choruses. The Spiritual Baptist songs are with African rhythms and sweet melodies. This I embrace in all my daily life and preach to all those who I come into contact with. I have been preaching the Spiritual Baptist Faith for thirty-five years and will continue my endeavours to share the richness it possesses. I enjoy mourning as a Spiritual Baptist; it is about a closer walk with God. It also means death and resurrection. Westward is death for three days. Eastward is resurrection to rise. This is a deep cleansing ritual, and one can develop a spiritual, mystical plane.

We now have churches all over the world that are doing charitable work and spiritual preaching and teaching. Today we have fourteen ministers and seven churches that I oversee. We are in the city of Toronto, in the province of Ontario, the country of Canada. We brought our rich culture and religious rights with us from the Caribbean and the African Diaspora. With our mandate, we serve the community as a whole. Once we were downtrodden and oppressed, and our dignity and self-esteem was taken away from us. Now we have reclaimed our dignity, self-esteem, and pride as Shouter Spiritual Baptists from the Caribbean and the African Diaspora.

ALONG THE WAY

A<small>S A SPIRITUAL</small> leader and counsellor, these are my values:

- I believe in the power of self-development, spiritual freedom, humanity, culture, love, and peace to all.
- I believe in using my power, motivation, and insight to rule and make decisions in a fair and graceful manner.
- I love being the peacemaker

I will share with you some personal affirmation that I use daily. Please feel free to use them in your lives as well.

- I love me, and I am the master of all I do.
- I am complete and beautiful, inside and out.
- I am what I am, because I believe in me.
- I love others.
- I show light in myself and all around me.
- I am totally at peace inside me.
- I am young and strong
- I am older and have strength. My energy is great.
- I am truly blessed. No one can take this away.
- I am so grateful for the abundance of things.

Pen and paper alone cannot express my gratitude toward God, but telling my story will give you the vitality to reach out to friends as you read about my daily journey. This special friend, God, is aware of our anxieties and the cares of life. He knows full well the purpose in which we get perplexed (Matthew 6:32-33), and He will supply your needs and my needs daily. There is hope as God searches for you and me; our hearts represent humanity with Christ. As I sit at the table and eat a meal, my meal is sustenance for my body just as God's love is sustenance for my spirit. These are the things that sustain me: my attitude, my relationships, my spiritual walk, my faith, and God's power.

My personal experiences, as well as other effective food for my body, are very important to my growth. After a full meal, the food is digested and assimilated, carrying strength to every fibre of my body. Nurturing my body keeps me healthy and vigorous; however, I always acquire fresh food daily. Spiritually and materially speaking, the table is spread. I sit down and discover the strength in my words. This book will be your strength from my words. The mystery of life is untold by many. In this moment as you read on, the mystery of my life is unfolded to be shared with great people like you.

I always like to separate the church from my personal life, but it seems it's always just a thought, because I am always in the public, and I've always felt comfortable with myself. For this reason, whatever I do or say will be reflected in my heart for the ministry.

As I develop in the faith, I also develop wisdom, knowledge, and understanding. For me to attain such heights, I had to keep humble, remain in devotion daily, and live a peaceful and holy life. It was also important for me to understand the real meaning of the hymns and psalms and develop a prophetic ear and voice.

Finally, my way of life has taught me that religion is just a man-made institution. To be unique, I like to identify with the inner being and know what it is that carries out here on earth to help anyone along the way, including members of my own household. The ability to reach this far with greater spiritual power must be attributed to the Spiritual Baptist Faith, because of the freedom to worship, the growth in the activities, and the strength in those who believed I could carry the banner with pride.

I pray and give praises to my God by His names Jehovah Jireh, Elohim, the El Elyon, the Great I Am, the El Shaddai, and the Lord of the supreme Jesus, Kings of kings.

To the ancestors and all those who know of my work on television and radio, in the churches. May the almighty Yahweh; archangels; and prophetic priests, queens, and kings continue to bless all those who read and listen to me. I was called by God do His will according to my gifts. Therefore I am driven by the Spirit, I eat, sleep, and work the spirit in my field of teaching, visiting the sick, performing weddings and funerals, preaching, healing, and hearing the prophetic voice/discernments.

As my quest continues in spirituality, I am aware of the Holy Spirit, the Elohim, "the creators," the divine intervention for all Faith—one Lord, one Faith, one Baptism.

PRAYER

WHAT KEEPS MY life going is prayer. I wrote a prayer book in 2001 called *Thoughts & Prayers from the Heart*, so you can tell how much I love to pray. My spiritual mother called me the prayer warrior, and I do believe in the power of prayer.

- Time to relax, let my business and personal life be effective, and reflect on myself.
- Time to spend in fasting (mourning, as per Spiritual Baptist Rites) for seven or fourteen days—no food, only water. This is silent time spent talking to God; purifying my body, my mind, and my soul; and clearing my heart and my chakras.
- Let God work in my life for the benefit of the community.
- Prayer for money management, property abundance, and paying off debts.
- Prayer for health, strength, and wealth.
- Prayer for wisdom, to set goals, to participate in programs, and to see the good in the youth.
- Prayer for travelling time and wellness. Meditation at six o'clock in the morning, noon, and six o'clock in the evening is a key to healing.

- Devotional mornings are for purification of the mind, clarity, and meetings to attend.
- Preaching was the key to my life, and there is time to win souls for the Kingdom of God. Therefore, prayer time is essential.
- The prosperity of the church and the needs of the membership needs prayer time.
- Prayer for the people and special thanks is given at all prayers.
- In every contract that is signed and every appointment that is attended, prayer is the focus before I make any decision. When travelling or recruiting, I ask for the unseen eye, and this is all done through prayer.

From my childhood, I learned to pray with mother, father, and family. In my youth, I learned to give thanks and pray for guidance. In my young adult life, if God had not been my help and if prayer had not been my food, I would not be alive. In my adult life, prayer sustains me and covers me in everything I say and do. Thanks be to God! At nearly every function I attend, I open or close in prayer if I am not the speaker. Through my prayer life, the gift of healing is manifested.

Throughout my travel experience, I return to Jamaica yearly, if possible, to visit my family. Because my husband was Barbadian, I visit Barbados as well. I travel to Trinidad and Tobago yearly due to my ministry, and there I attend the liberation for the Spiritual Baptist. I visit various parts of the United States due to family, as well as England to visit a friend. During this period as I travelled to London, England, my husband died. It was very sad, and the children understood the mission that I took. I came back and had to do a lot of legal work and clean up personal things. Again, my prayer life made this happen.

A Gift from the Spirit

I T WAS A beautiful, sunny day, and the phone rang. It was a man looking for Deloris Seiveright, the archbishop. I said, "This is her speaking."

The person was interested in knowing more about the Baptists in Toronto—the services, the programs, etc. The conversation was very professional to the point that he gave me his first and last name. He was coming to Toronto on February 19 and said he would stop by to talk to me about the church and the program. He mentioned that he had seen me on the Internet and was moved with other interests, of which he would let me know of when he saw me. He also mentioned he had help for other people and had various spiritual connections.

He came, I saw, we greeted, he drank, we sat down, and he spoke in length about his vision and places he has been. I personally did not hear half of what he was saying. I was listening, but I was reading him as well. I asked him, "What do you want?"

He talked around the question and said he would write a proposal and give me ideas. All I saw was the attraction—the connection of spiritual activities between us. I was also amazed that I picked up his past life and asked him about it. He admitted to it but said he had changed in some ways. He mentioned either that he was going to a spiritual retreat or just coming from one with another faith. I was surprised, because my observation was that this man wanted to know more about the Spiritual Baptist Faith and Deloris. He left for the day.

He called me the next day, but he sounded a bit confused and depressed. I spoke to him several times, and he was uplifted. I saw our relationship as a spiritual and platonic one, but I was struggling with a sense of deeper inner feelings that I tried to dismiss. He came back to see me again. This time, it was during a work conference in Toronto. It was now March. I invited him to a function hosted by a fellow minister friend named Earl. He offered to pick me up and take me so that I wouldn't have to drive. I returned home by midnight. He went back to his hotel, and we spoke on the phone that night until one o'clock the next morning.

It was like having a good piece of cookie in my mouth. Our telephone bills escalated, as he lived in Ottawa. When I travelled to Trinidad, we spoke. When I came back, we saw each other every weekend. He accompanied me to various functions where I introduced him to different people. We travelled; I visited his home, and he visited my church. He was eventually baptized in the faith and mourned. He soon realised that I could not handle this amount of work by myself. He was in awe of the amount of work I had to do. Not knowing if he could help, he offered to try to help in any way that he could.

One day he told me that he would like to stay with me and be together as husband and wife. I said, "You're crazy!" The first thing was that the age difference was a problem for me. He had no children, and I was finished having mine. We spoke in length about it. We looked at all that affected us or would be affected by us, including work, our homes, our families, the church, and religion. Anything you can think of—you name it, we discussed it.

For him, the age did not matter. After all, "we were not that far apart," he said. He had no problem accepting my children as his own. The challenge was that he had asked me to move where he was, because he had a good, steady job. I could not. All that I had built was in Toronto. I told him, "You can come here if you really, really want me. If not, then you're probably still married anyhow."

As soon as he hung up the phone, he e-mailed me his divorce paper. He came down to Toronto, and we saw a lawyer where we discussed things like finances. Then we went to the government office and picked up our certificate of marriage. I called my sons and gave them the news. They were so excited. We got married with my son, my family, and two witnesses present.

Stephen went back to Ottawa to organize how he was going to move down, quit his job, and start his new life in Toronto. Our marriage has bloomed, as we adjusted the best we could. During the transition, we have lost some friends and gained better ones. My relatives are happy for me, and my family loves him. We are great. God is in our lives.

Since November 2009, my life has made a 180-degree turn. A sudden reality has hit home. My life has changed for the better, but within these very happy moments, I'm also very nervous. Stephen moved in November. After living by myself for so long, I now had to get used to making space for things like his clothes, furniture, boxes, suitcases, different types of food, and the list goes on. The main change was getting use to not driving myself around in my car but instead being driven by my husband. I had to get used to not being by myself. Adjusting to sleeping with someone else in the bed was a lovely change, but also challenging. I was used to never having to cook if I didn't want to, sleeping when I wanted, and just doing what I wanted, when I want.

I'm a praying person. I love to pray, so we pray together, talk about spiritual things, go to church together, work with each other, bless each other, watch TV together, and love each other. We know for a fact that there are a lot of people who do not understand our union and come off as being upset by it. Inquiring minds want to know more about our union, but there's nothing to know. We are like most—a happily married couple enjoying life together. When we sense negative vibrations, we deflect them with our positive spirits. As for me, I just focus and keep going. God has accepted our decision, and hopefully the world will too. The congratulations from those who are happy for us in the community and church have been enjoyable and overwhelming.

For romance, cherish the love of your life, whether it lasts a few months, a few years, many years, or a lifetime. Days after you look back, you will see the joy of being you, and moments of joy will cover you in times of sadness or despair.

Love is beyond our human comprehension. It becomes overwhelming the more I strive to understand love and the immensity I have for God's infinite love. There is no reason to lose hope over the course of various instances, because love surmounts all of my failures. The loving providence of God, our Father, saw my needs through the years, day by day. As one of His children, my heart is overwhelmed with awareness and joy as He speaks to me along life's way. For this reason, I listen to His voice, and I hear His awesome words coming from the throne of God. His union with me reaches my heart, dismissing all fear, and replaces it with perfect love.

YOUTH PASSION

SHOUTERS GREW EVEN more when we moved to Scarborough. The hand of God was upon us. Another vision came, and it was to help the youth. I met Mr. L, a youth who knew how to go about this plan. I created my first youth program at our Kennedy location with the help of Father Cruise, who was from an Anglican Church. Thanks be to God! As I worked to get the program started, I met great people along the way. I was energetic and ready to work the hardest to do what it took to help the community, especially the youth.

One bright summer evening (with the sun out in Toronto, it was about 31 degrees Celsius), I took a walk and sat in the shade under a tree in the park. I had my usual spiritual book, *The Desert Stream*, from which I read daily spiritual thoughts. I saw a group of young men talking, but they seemed angry with passion as they communicated with each other. I was not sure if it was business or pleasure. I said a bright "hello" to them, although I didn't know if they saw or heard me. I came home to my sons and told them what I'd seen.

They said, "Mom, that is the life out there."

I had to question myself. My sons taught and coached me as they informed me of what the youth face daily with their peers. When I think back, some of my sons' peers were afraid to come to the door of our house. When they did, I always had a long list of questions for them: "Are you in school? Which school? Does your mother know you are here? How are your grades? Why do you dress like that? Why do you speak like that? Do you have a girlfriend? Do you go to church?"

My sons would get very upset for questioning their friends so much. I always knew that the lives of the youth would be rough without some spiritual or moral counselling.

With the help of my growing sons, I plunged into the community with the vision to help the youth by getting to them early. Saving even one would be an accomplishment. I was one of the first founding clergy who helped to organize a Black Clergy Association, due the crime and violence. I can recall an earlier vision of myself preaching at the subway to people on the street. The need was great! When we called a vigil, only a few people came out to pray. Thanks to the other founding clergy members, we held meetings over and over again, looking for ideas or solutions. To this day, the same things always pop up—youth values, their parents, their schools, and the list goes on.

The youth project came off with great success. We would pick up youth from all over Toronto. We had opened a permanent youth outreach program.

These words are from my two sons: "We were just kids the other day. My brother and I are now seeing our Mother finish twenty-seven years of progress. I know retirement does not stop your progress. You're a fighter. Love, Jez and Josiah."

These words from a youth leave an indelible mark in my mind. When a mother's coaching and teaching are there, her children speak well of them always. Whenever possible, thank your children. I love you both, Jezreel and Josiah.

I have been running youth programs since 1991 and have interacted with more than 350 youth. Through these programs, I have experienced a surmounting disappointment in both boys and girls, especially black and ethnic youth. It has been said, and sometimes it's true, that the system has upset and stereotyped our sons and daughters. They get caught up in the mix with little or no hope.

That being said, I also see the girls, as well as a few boys, excelling in university and am proud that the nurturing has helped some. I hope and pray for those who have been less successful. Our government has completed various reports on the youth, showing that poverty, poor housing, and lack of parental guidance all help to create low self-esteem in youth. I choose to develop programs that invest in education, skill development, and hope, which all work together to create a good quality of life. The effectiveness of these programs depends on parental involvement, great youth workers, time taken to encourage and train, and a genuine voice to say "I care."

The youth have great knowledge. When equipped with the right resources, they can soar like eagles. They are human and need friendship and love. Once they see the hope and experience the caring, they will tell friends what helped them. That might be a program, or it might just a person like myself.

I invest in them by telling my story. I use myself as a mediator, as a mentor, as a coach. Most really see me as a mother who's not living with them. Some love my motherhood, while others love me as the mediator. With my experience and continued investment in training programs, I believe that there can be less crime. However, I must say that we do have a few who are too far gone, and only the divine can help them. I love the youth; they are my children. I wish I could say to each one of them: "I love you all with that unconditional love. You can reach the stars and achieve anything you desire." For the youth reading this book, I'd like to them, "Get an education. With it you can overcome the barriers and take charge of your life. May God bless you, so you can bless others when you reach my age."

A note to parents: be in charge, but let your children fly. Do not clip their wings. Give them encouragement to have faith and strength, to know the truth, and to live the values you placed in the home, church, mosque, chapel, temple, meditation circle, or community gatherings. Learn from your children. Be firm and strong; give the tough love but have that peace that passeth all understanding. Parents, the respect you give will come back to you many times over. Parents are not perfect, but with wisdom, we can grow and nurture our youth to be good men and women of tomorrow.

As I write, I pray for the community and hope that people's minds can attest to my experiences and knowledge. My greatest wish is to see the youth reconciled with themselves—for each youth to "know thyself."

Some of my most challenging and rewarding experiences have been with young people. Some handled their issues with silence, while others were very vocal. Some resorted to a state of depression to the point of not being able to function at all. Age had no limit. For example, one of the youth I saw was so depressed that his parents thought he was going mad. When I spoke to the youth during a session, I found that the whole idea of the rebellious behaviour stemmed from the perception that his parents loved his sibling more. Yes, they had given most of their attention to their other child. In this case, the parents blamed their child for not succeeding. Some parents yell and scream at their children when they don't live up to their expectations. The result in this case was that the youth moved to an aunt's home where he received more attention than his parents gave him. The youth excelled, but he continues to work on feelings of anger toward his parents.

It takes both parents to realise that their love toward their children may not be balanced. Some parents are not apologetic to their children. It is often said that children must obey their parents. In order for children to obey, they must also receive love, because they need it. Love is not money, material things, or food. It is giving attention, speaking with each other, hugging, playing, laughing together, sitting at the dining room table together, and spending quality time as a family. It is very sad that this youth never went back home because he felt that there was no love there. This is why there are so many young people out in the cold and on the streets seeking love. Unfortunately, there are people who disagree with me.

In another case, I knew of a young single mother who worked and went to school, not returning home until eleven o'clock at night. Her daughter cooked for the family every day when the mother went off to work. The woman's son, on the other hand, sat in front of the television all day and invited friends over. Every morning the mother asked the two children how school was going. They would both answer that they were fine. She would then do chores and head off to work again. This was the routine for years.

One day the school called, because the son had been expelled. The mother quickly accused the "wicked society," stating that the system was bad. She had not taken a look at herself yet. Fortunately for the woman, her daughter stayed out of trouble and was a good student. Her son came to me for counselling. During our time together, he pointed out that he would not see his mother for days on end, because she was always busy working. I came to find out that the boy did leave notes from school for his mom to view and told her that the teacher wanted to speak with her. In response to her son, she would say that she would get to it later or was too busy to view the notes. The boy did not seek the help of the school guidance counsellor, because his friends told him that it wouldn't help and was a waste of time.

I made an appointment with the guidance counsellor and informed the boy's mother, and all three of us attended the appointment together. During the meeting, I had to politely ask the boy's mother to stop talking and listen. After all, she did not take the time to sit and speak before the meeting, so why should she speak to no end now? The meeting had come to an end regarding the young boy's future. Within a couple of days, the guidance counsellor allowed the boy to finish school. The young boy graduated and went on to further his future at college. Some parents are so busy that they do not recognize when their children are seeking their direction.

In another case, a very bright young lady could not get good grades. Her teacher advised her that she would need special lessons, and her parents would be informed. Her parents were informed, but they were too busy to address her needs. This left the girl in tears. Her parents were familiar with the school system, so I suggested extra lessons with their daughter's teacher. However, the problem existed between the teacher and the student. The young girl had low self-esteem, which caused her to believe she could not make it through school.

With my counselling sessions and encouragement, the young girl got a new teacher and excelled, even graduating with honours. The school system has some teachers who need to look beyond skin and gender and teach their students without any bias. The system has failed some children, but thanks to community leaders with passions like me and parents who listen and take time to love, more and more students are graduating and beating the system. Statistics show that young people have barriers. The youth of today are looking for programs that will help them find financial aid for school, help them with skill development, and help them find some kind of work. Youth seeking change in their lives also come to me for counselling.

There was the case of a crown's child who grew up not knowing her biological parents. She only knew foster parents and grew up moving from home to home. She shoplifted from the ages of thirteen to seventeen and found herself charged with a crime. She came to me seeking help.

After many sessions of counselling, she was able to get her own place, go back to school, and move on to being a better person. Six months later I received a call that the young lady was arrested for theft, fraud, and money laundering, I was so very sad. She is still incarcerated until this very day. Is this an isolated case? Can we do better, I wonder, and how?

The next case I am going to tell you about is no surprise. A young man from our youth program, along with his friends, was caught with drugs and guns. He called me first, even before he called his lawyer.

"Yes, Miss Dr. Seiveright, I am in jail," the young man said after I answered the telephone.

I said, "What for? What did you do?" He said it was a long story but explained that he hadn't done anything wrong. He was just with his friends who had drugs and guns. "What did you have?" I asked him.

He answered, "Nothing. Nothing. I was just with them."

When I asked if he had informed his parents, he said that he hadn't yet. He did not want them to know right away, because he was afraid that they would kill him. He asked me to contact his lawyer. I did this hastily, knowing that it was Friday and he would be locked up all weekend if he didn't get a lawyer soon. I contacted the mother, who fainted initially when I told her the news. She stayed in contact with the lawyer.

"Thank you very much, Dr Seiveright," the boy told me. "Please pray for me, and I will see you when I come out."

"But you don't know when you are going to get out," I replied.

Confident, he answered, "When you get me a lawyer, I will be out."

His parents and I attended the hearing that morning, and the young man was granted bail. I worked with his probation officer and lawyer and gave references to his behaviour in my program. After his experience with the legal system, the young man went back to college after being on parole for two years. He changed his life around, changed his friends, and moved on to better things.

Trust me, the fainthearted cannot work with these youth. My strength and endurance must come from God. From my perspective, there are young men out there who need direction and encouragement. They can do better with help and good resources. Let me say this: There are some who do not get it. Their lives are still in a circle, in and out, round and about. However, there are some who struggle but succeed in the end with the help of good friends, a good home, participating parents, community leaders, and programs such as Shouters to help them.

A lot of youth don't get a place to catch a break and excel. Often youth come into our programs with no sense of direction. When they first arrive, I ask them, "What do you want to do with your life? Start a business? What kind of business?"

"I have some business ideas, but I'm not sure. I want to be my own boss," one answered.

"Do you live at home?" I asked.

"No," he responded

"Do you live on your own?"

"No."

"Then who do you live with?" I questioned.

"I live with some friends," he said.

"Do you work?" I asked

"Yes, but I do not have a steady job. When I get a call, I help," he responded.

"Did you finish high school?"

"I have one more subject to get my diploma," he explained.

"Okay, fill out the forms, and I will see what I can do for you," I told him.

"Please, Dr Seiveright, I really want to do something. Can I get in?" he questioned. "Will you call me back?"

"Yes," I assured him. "I will call you in three to seven days."

I did call within three to seven days with good news that he had been accepted into the program. He came to the first workshop, and the first thing we discussed was his education. He said he was distracted at school but would finish our program.

I could already see the success in his eyes and hear the determination in his voice. I paired him up with a mentor to work on his self-esteem, time management, dress code, presentation, and verbal skills. I was proud of him—within six months, his business was up and running. He had clientele, was networking, and was never afraid to look for what he wanted. When he made his first profit, he took me out for tea and a bagel to thank me for all my help. He bought a car, has his own office space, and still continues to succeed. And he achieved all of this before his twenty-fifth birthday. His success just fills my eyes with tears of joy.

As a leader, mother, and citizen, I cannot give up on our youth. There are people who can climb the ladder of success. I will always let young people know they have a place in my heart. My two sons always say, "Mom, you don't have just two sons. You have many children in Toronto." I give my love to the parents of our youth and advise them to work hard while still giving time and love to their children.

Youth should make sure to give back to the community, live life with a passion, do what's best for themselves, and be good role models in our society. Do all you can and save this affirmation. I live by it. If I can serve one person, I will save one individual.

Adult Counselling

I 'VE PREACHED AT many churches, done healing services, held services in the park, and prayed at many functions, but a major part of my life involves counselling people. In the nineties, I took a Christian and marriage counselling course. After studying cases of people's behaviour, I've come to realise that every case, situation, and problem is unique and different. I've met so many people from all walks of life, and the issues of each person whom I've counselled are as different as each person is from another. In the end, however, they all just want to talk to someone. These counselling sessions are experiences that I will always embrace.

One perk of my ministry is performing marriage ceremonies. I enjoy seeing God shared between two people as they join together. The reality of marriage is that it requires the work of both parties. For just as much as I enjoy working with youth, I must say I also enjoy working with married couples. I will venture to let you know about two cases I encountered in my marriage counselling sessions.

A man and a woman came in for premarital counselling. Due to my spiritual insights, I was able to let the couple know that they would get married and live together, but their marriage would not last unless they got their financial problems sorted out.

"Yes, yes, yes. We know that. It is not a problem," the couple replied in unison.

After a long period of counselling sessions, the couple got married. Two months into the marriage, the husband got hold of his wife's credit card. He bought a new car and several other personal items with the card. Within five to six months of marriage, the couple got divorced, leaving the wife to pay off her husband's debt. Later on, the wife called to tell me I was right, as she explained what had taken place.

Some may wonder why they got married in the first place. They had to learn their own lessons, I guess. They were adamant about being together and were in love at the time. Love can really put a blindfold on people and cover bad finances or habits. Unfortunately, this couple could not see beyond their wedding day.

Another couple who had been married for twenty years wanted to end their relationship. They came to talk to me about their separation. I asked them several questions, the main one being, "Why do you want to separate?"

"He sleeps, snores, and does nothing," the wife replied.

"She nags, nags, talks, and says nothing that makes sense. She does the same thing over and over again," her husband replied. The man was fifty years old, and his wife was fifty-three. They had grown together and had come to know each other. So, I arranged to do four sessions over a couple of months. At first, I had private sessions with each spouse.

The results were in. This couple had grown their now successful children, and in the process, they had come to realise that they had been putting all their valuable time into their children and not themselves as a couple. They did not have sexual relations frequently, and when they did, it was after one of them begged the other. The only affection given in their relationship was the occasional kiss on the cheek. Movie nights would result in both of them falling asleep.

"You're only in your fifties. Life now begins," I told them. I realised I had some work to do.

In the private sessions, I instructed the wife to buy new lingerie and a new dress. I told the husband to buy a new suit. By this time, I knew they had not done this in about thirty-five years. I instructed them to the doctor and have a physical performed, have a night out to a theatre, go straight to a hotel after, and make love, not have intercourse, instead of falling asleep. The couple went away, and we reconvened our session in three weeks.

They did go out of town. The wife informed me that when they got to the hotel, her husband said he was too tired, so they went to the movies. When they got back from the movies, they made love. She was so bright. The progress was causing them to get excited. Our session ended with a balance in both their lives and marriage. Their love continues to grow in various ways. They communicate well and live life to its fullest. Well! I was in laughter and full of joy with the newfound couple.

Cases like this are very common. Married couples forget their first love. They come in to talk to me about one problem and discover many underlying problems. Some are not feeling well, some are going through life changes, some are seeking comfort elsewhere, and some lack in sex drive. Spouses should see a medical doctor to ensure they have no health issues, talk to a genuine friend, go back to a life of dating their spouse, regenerate, live, love, and laugh.

May I continue to nourish, give advice, and help to change even one life.

A Natural Gift

I N 2003 I decided to start my own business. Can you imagine? I was preaching, teaching, and running the church, and now I wanted to add a business to the list!

As a new entrepreneur, I created programs and taught extra classes in meditation, counselling, and mentorship. I wrote three books—a prayer book, a study book, and a compiled hymn book—and I produced two CDs. I realised the sale of the CDs and books did not keep me or the church financially stable. I had to use my passion wisely, so I did ordinations, established churches, performed marriages, and authorized ministers in the archdiocese. I blessed homes and drove to all kinds of events to network. I met people from all walks of life from Parliament Hill to the beggars and homeless. I did a lot of motivational work, as I have mentioned, and attended conferences in the United States and Toronto as guest speaker.

Invitations to speak have led me to meet many people and experience wonderful times. My most memorable invite happened in 2003. I was invited to Edmonton to speak at a conference by the Jamaican Association of Northern Alberta. All my lodging was prepared. They were very caring, loving, and informative. They took me around Alberta, showed me the different activities, and took me to the West Edmonton mall. I wanted to know where I was going to stay, and I soon realised that they were taking a long time to tell me. They kept calling around and telling me that the room was not ready.

Finally, they took me to a house where they told me I would be staying. When the person approached the door, I was surprised and just about fainted. It was my girlfriend from Toronto who I'd known since the eighties. She had moved to Edmonton and gotten married. We were both in shock. She was one of the first directors of my organization. We hugged and hugged and hugged and then chatted and laughed. Then we tried to figure out how this had all happened. She said that when they told her a guest speaker was coming and that it was me, she immediately offered to put me up. She wanted it to be a surprise, so no one was supposed to tell me where I'd be staying. After our visit, we all got some rest and then got ready for the function. The next day we visited a friend; enjoyed shared laughter, food, and music; and went shopping. I returned to Toronto at eleven o'clock that night. Edmonton was awesome, and Alberta is a beautiful place.

On May 17, 2002, I got a ride to the airport to board Air Canada flight 175 on route to Winnipeg, Manitoba. It was 9:30 a.m., and there was a welcome reception for the group from the National Council. The reception was held at the JCA Cultural Centre in Manitoba. All Jamaicans were there, as though we were outside in a backyard in Jamaica. Men and women were playing dominos, the liquor was flowing like water, young people were playing basketball, and everyone was speaking English and Patois mixed together. Only private introductions were made to us.

We all went back to the hotel, and one lady didn't have a room booked. What chaos! We finally got a ride to the Viscount Hotel. Believe me, no one was smiling by this time. I was supposed to share a room with a lady named Ms P. She came off the fourth floor, went to sleep somewhere else, and then sent the lady who didn't have a room to my room. The room number was 606. I was up all night, because the lady in my room was snoring. I had a headache, but I finally went to bed at three o'clock in the morning and got two hours sleep.

I woke up at five thirty and was dressed by seven o'clock. Ms P came back to our room to join us. The snoring lady was doing paperwork. I was so hungry, but I was reading over my speech, because I had to speak at the conference before lunch. The three of us finally went down for breakfast, and the session started. I spoke for fifteen minutes on my life growing up, how I was nurtured, what I studied, and what I experienced coming to Canada. I told the group how youth could move and do anything they put their minds to.

As a gift, I received a dark polar bear engraved with my name and the organization. I went to the mall after we were done and then made my reservation for the airport. Three ladies went with me to the mall from; they were from Windsor, Alberta, and Ottawa. We all bought something, except the one from Alberta. I returned to the hotel, showered, got a massage, rested, and packed. I really needed to pray, and so I did.

At the banquet, I said the grace. I met the deputy mayor of Winnipeg and the Member of Provincial Parliament for the Ministry of Labour and Tourism, as well as delegates from Jamaica and all over. At 11:30 p.m., everyone was on the dance floor. I danced for a minute and then left for the lounge. I had not taken my dancing shoes with me. I sat with three ladies, but one left for the slot machine. I returned to my room at about 1:30 a.m.

Everyone else came up later. Amazingly, we had three people in the room. I'm not sure how the plans changed from two to three, intentionally or on accident. We spoke for a while before going to bed, and the snoring continued. I woke up at four o'clock in the morning and got a cab for the airport. I got on Air Canada flight 190 en route to Toronto. One of the mothers from the church picked me up, drove me home, and took me to church on Sunday.

After church, I slept for four hours, got up, and went back to bed until Monday morning at nine o'clock. When I finally woke up, I ate corned beef and bread for breakfast. I decided to wash my hair, call my family, and cook chicken. I planned to make other calls to tell everyone that I had come back from the hills and survived. Next, I called a friend in Cuba, cut the grass, and saw my grandchildren and sons. This was the day I reflected on my travelling experience—the hills, the mountains, and the smell of Manitoba.

During this time, church membership increased by more than 50 percent. I really wanted a church building, and being determined, I would sacrifice what I could. As a matter of fact, I continue to give more than one-tenth to the church. I was working really hard, but when I left Bell, my income was cut in half. I was living below the poverty line. Back then, my mortgage was low, so I remortgaged my home twice in order to survive.

I sought financial advice, and everyone I spoke to advised me to remortgage my home. I have a great friend who went to be with the Lord in 2008; he always told me that I was going to burn myself out. He helped me out by managing my finances and separated the churches finances from my personal affairs. He even drove me himself to Consumers Road in Toronto and Canada Revenue Agency to incorporate my business as a not-for-profit organization. He was a great help.

I had once thought the world was okay without Deloris, but I have come to realise that I'm important and in demand. I received calls requesting me to perform weddings and funerals, give speeches at various functions, and pray, lecture, or do workshops. This is the world that I truly cared for. I love speaking. I have preached for more than twenty-one years, given 756 sermons, said 210 public prayers, made speeches, given lectures, and held seminars. However, my communication skills did not come overnight. It has been a work in progress since my childhood.

I used to be very quiet, but I always observed people who spoke well, remembering every little thing that took place. I wanted to exhale the quiet communication within me; therefore, I found a group known as Toastmasters. There, I was trained how speak publicly and improve my timing and oration skills. I thought it was impossible to speak for five, ten, or fifteen minutes and amazed myself when I would accomplish it. I can certainly speak clearly, be concise, and still deliver the message in a short time.

Whether I speak to small or large crowds, I love the energy of sharing my inner thoughts on spirituality. Spirituality is my niche and another subject that I will write about. If I am unexpectedly called upon to speak at a function, I'm always ready to do so. However, like with most things, preparation in advance helps me to perform even better. Sometimes I write my speeches, but most of the time, I speak from my heart. My sermons are inspired through the divine guidance of the Holy Spirit.

In writing this book, as I do with anything, I have used meditation and quiet devotion to get my thoughts together. Before I get ready to speak or preach, I say these words, my mantra or affirmation, "Let the light be in my heart, in my ears, in my eyes, on my right, on my left, above me, and beneath me. Let the light surround me, be with me, and let me be the light as I speak or write, that all who hear and read will be inspired, will be moved by the power of my words." Another great way I prepare myself is to use the three Ls, Ps, or Ts, which stand for love, light, live; personality, prosperity, people; and talk, teach, and take. I've learned to talk the walk and teach the walk and then take what I teach for myself to help me to re-evaluate my life and my daily walk with God.

Speaking may be a love of mine, but other joys of my ministry are performing funerals, baby christenings, and weddings. The grieving, the hurt, and the reaction to the loss of a loved one require someone to give hope and comfort. I've sat with family members who are afraid of the abandonment and are anxious. They cannot function with the attachment and their expression of love for the deceased. They are grieving. This is where I step in.

I tell the truth, listen, respond to their needs, try to be sensitive and available, make suggestions, protect the family member from vulnerability, and provide spiritual health and support. Unfortunately, most funerals lead to people fighting over land, insurance money, and the will. Family members don't communicate, and no one has enough money to move the process along.

There are two good things about funerals—the person who has passed will rest forever, and family members reunite, despite the grieving, by sharing great songs, eating great food, hugging, crying, leaning on each other, and supporting one another. My message at funeral services is always for the attendees of the funeral in hope that some people will give their lives to God and re-evaluate their current situations.

Baby christenings are done with care and protection. The child must be anointed to grow and live in the world with a guardian angel. Therefore, the dove of peace and protection must be invoked with that Divine power and the Holy Spirit of God. The power of the blessed water will consecrate the child in his or her future life. A child placed in my arms for blessings will go out in the world with spiritual protection.

I have performed more than 130 weddings since 1984 as a licensed minister. I know the joy of love and marriage and extend my heart to the couples in front of me. I encourage them to enjoy their moment of splendour—the moment when two hearts are as one.

When anyone tells me that I am good, with humility, I say that I am as good as I can be. I give my best at all times. I have found that when one is anointed by the Holy Spirit through the Divine Creator, there is no place for mediocrity. God is powerful, and His servants must have power.

For me, my ability to speak or preach is a gift given by God. When I'm filled with the spirit, my voice changes, and I sometimes become louder or softer. The message stays on point, remains consistent, and is enough to clarify the minds of the people in the audience. I am grateful for the purpose and the passion I have to speak and write.

2002 to 2009 are years to remember as growth in spirit and also in community work. I celebrated twenty-five years in ministry with a celebration organized by my daughter-in law. It was raining, and everyone was waiting for me at Q-Siss Banquet Hall. Among those that attended were government delegates, community leaders, church leaders, friends, and parishioners. The video, dancers, and entertainers were great.

WOMAN OF HER TIME— TILL WE MEET AGAIN

O N MAY 10, 2009, I received a call from Mama telling me that she would be going for a few weeks from her home Hyde to Falmouth to stay at Dennis's residence. My mother thought it would only be for two weeks, but her stay went on for six months. My siblings in Jamaica thought this was the best thing for Mama. I called and called but was told that because I no longer lived there, decisions should be left for them to make. I called again, and everyone in Jamaica said Mom was doing fine. She could not hear too well, because she was ninety-eight, but she knew I had called. I loved my mom so much and missed talking to her, so I planned to go home soon. It was October when I finally spoke to Mom. She asked me when I was coming. I said I'd be there soon. She replied, "Okay. I will wait until you come." I knew then that I would see Mom again.

There had been so much fuss about Mom before my sister Clover and I arrived back home to visit her. Our siblings had planned to have her back at her home by this time. While in Toronto, I had been very vocal that Mom should have never left her home for so long. The claim was that there was no one to take care of her, and my brother Calvin, who lived with her, needed a break. My statement did not go over well with most of the family.

I spoke to Dennis and explained my feelings and suggestions. He said that he knew what he had done was right and best for Mom, so I trusted his judgement. Although I had heard him, I did not totally agree with everything. It was my understanding that Calvin's wife had been at home to take care of Mom, but she no longer had time since she had started running a store. I spoke to Calvin and his wife. They said very little and had left everything about the situation in the hands of the Lord.

I decided to get a personal take of the situation, as I had promised Mom to come back home to visit. I arrived on November 13, 2009. Clover had been there a day before me. I waited for more than two hours for Calvin to pick me up at the airport only to hear that it was too late to get Mom back home. I said there was no way I was going to the home without her and called Dennis to let him know that I was coming to get her. She was so happy that we'd come to get her. She waited up for us. My mother was so happy, and I was overemotional. Clover and I stayed all week in her room with her. We went to church on Sunday and then went home and cooked. She was so happy. We spent a lovely day with Mom.

The rest of the time was spent sitting and chatting with Mom. She desperately wanted to just stay at her home and begged us to stay with her there. I will never forget that. We told her to ask her sons if she could stay at her home. So she turned to Calvin and asked him to hire someone to care for her. I remember her bowels being really loose. We prayed and worked with her, washed her, and got her ready. We took Mom back to Dennis's the next Thursday evening. Before Mom got into the car, my husband called. Mom spoke with Stephen and told him to take care of her daughter.

"I love her very much, so you must love my daughter very much," she told him. Mom cried and cried as we left. We prayed and prayed. Hugs and kisses.

Three weeks later I got a call from home informing me that Mom had a stroke. She was found on the floor near the bed. It was December 17, 2009, at 10:30 a.m. Dennis spoke to Calvin, his wife, Georgia, Clover, and I about Mom's death. I was told Mom was not doing well weeks before she died. I also dreamt the night of December 16 that Mom was gone, and I could not see her or where she was. It was very sad. I spoke to Jezreel and Stephen, and we all were very sad. I was in a state of shock. Both of them spent the day with me. We called and talked about the planning for the funeral and when to fly down. We finalized the date for January 2, 2010.

I spoke to Josiah and his family in Florida. I called everyone whom I was able to call. Stephen and I went down on December 30, 2009. Jezreel stayed back and conducted the New Year's Eve service. Then he and my nephews flew in on January 1, 2010. We all stayed at Calvin's home. Saturday was a very busy day. We all went to the church service and then committed Mom's body at the family plot. Stephen videotaped the funeral for us. The rest of the week was spent meeting and greeting families while we travelled.

This experience taught me lessons about spiritual knowledge, strength, and living the greater life with love for all people. It also gave me joy for the love that I shared with my mother and family and for who I am. I give God thanks each day for the mother I had and will never forget that she taught me a lot of things, the most important being to serve God, pray all the time, and be at peace with myself. She taught me to dress well, to look good, to eat well, and to take very good care of myself.

Mother's prayerful life and singing have had a great impact on the way I live at home, at school, at church, and at work. She was a community person, and I can attest to that. Her way of life set a very high standard that I can attain. Dad died ten years before Mom passed. I miss him dearly also, but Mom stayed around for a longer time and will always be in my heart. Mom always let me know that she loved me dearly. She always told me to preach well, love the members, and keep the church going. Mom was always a straight talker with me, and her love was never limited. Her love was for all her children, grandchildren, and great-grandchildren, even those who were not related by blood. Her memory serves her well up to the last day of her life—a very Christian and spiritual mother to me and everybody around her. This chapter has closed on Mom's life on Earth but will never close with the divine spirit. Farewell, Mama Alice, Mom, Mother. Until we meet again.

MY FIRST CRUISE

I DECIDED TO TAKE another journey, this time a Mediterranean Cruise. I received a called from Ms D. "Hey, Arch, how would you like to go on a cruise?" she asked.

"Sure, I will go if it's free," I said.

She said, "Just tell me yes or no."

I said, "Yes." I gave her my information, I got prepared, and my son helped me pack with Ms O. When the time came, Ms O drove me to Ms D's house, and we went to the airport together. We took Sky service flight F65 0750 to Palma in seven and a half hours. We went to the tour ship, changed, and ate all we could. We watched the ship sail off to Bizerte, Tunisia, in Africa. We planned to tour Tunisia with another couple in Cabin 86. In Palma, many people were poor. We could see the poverty—the food was all over the market, and it wasn't as clean as we expected. I was amazed at myself how I sailed while suffering from ocean sickness, but the ocean was amazing. I looked at the ocean, observed the beauty of God, and said "wow."

On Monday we went to Civitavecchia, Italy. We had great food and wine; it was awesome. Then we went to Livorno, Florence, Italy, which had amazing structure and buildings. Shopping was beautiful, and the marketplace was awesome. There we saw the beautiful paintings by Michelangelo. We went to St. Peter's Basilica and the Vatican, where we saw the saints, the live tombs, where the Pope lived, and the artwork of Mussolini.

The next day we went to Ville Nice, France. We also went to Monaco, Monte Carlo, and Venice. We had to take a special tender to Nice, and then we were able to shop. However, Ms D and I did not know where we were to get the tender, so we split up, and I was on my own. I screamed, I cried, I balled, I hollered—I asked everyone the direction to the boat, but no one could understand me. I finally caught my composure and turned right, and there was the boat. I just caught the boat by five minutes. Ms D and I laughed and laughed—it was not funny and funny at the same time. We had the captain's ball that night; we were dressed to kill, very formal. We met the captain and different people; the beauty of the décor was amazing, and the food was very good. But Ms D was not well, so she went back to her cabin after a while. The next day we went to Barcelona. The streets were narrow, the shopping was exquisite, and the beauty of Spain was great.

May 31, 2002, was packing day. We went to the disco and listened to music, and as I always do, I prayed before bed. We woke up the next day, checked out of Palma (Mojora), went to the airport, and boarded Sky service flight 751 en route to Toronto. Travelling at 39,000 feet for 4,328 miles, it took us eight and a half hours. We returned to Toronto at 6:45 p.m. The landing was rough but safe. I took the airport limo home for seventy-five Canadian dollars. I came home as usual, gave thanks, and called my sons. That day my son was twenty years old. I rested, and then I went to church.

BADGE OF HONOUR

I TRAVELLED TO JAMAICA on October 14, 2011, and arrived in Montego Bay Airport. Stephen travelled on Air Canada, while I travelled on West Jet. We met in the baggage area, got our luggage, and changed eighty Canadian dollars into eight thousand Jamaican dollars. Then we proceeded to call Calvin, who said he was in Falmouth. We then took our time to walk to customs. When we were done, we went outside. By this time, it was two o'clock in the afternoon Jamaican time.

Next, we located the booth where we could get digital international and local minutes for my phone. When we got directions from the baggage handlers and taxi men, they told us to go outside, look near the tuxedo shop, and go inside. They said we'd see a booth, and a lady would give us minutes there for our phone card. Once we found the booth, we knocked on the door. It was locked. A man called to a lady and said, "See, people want to buy minutes!"

She came over, opened the door, and asked how much we wanted to spend. I told her that I wanted to spend JM$1000 for overseas calls and JM$400 for local minutes. So we gave her JM$1800 and got back JM$400. We then waited at the curb for Calvin. It was now 2:30 p.m.

I called him, and he said, "I'm comin'. I'm comin'." I called again and again. We waited for more than an hour. Then we waited in the sun, lots of sun, so we got a drink at the top shop. It cost JM$100. It was limeade, and it tasted like sugar and water. However, Stephen and I were very thankful for the juice. We just wanted some water, but we made it.

Finally, Calvin called and said he was two minutes away. It was 3:50 p.m. Since our 1:30 p.m. landing, it had been approximately two hours. We jumped in the car—I ran in the car—he welcomed us and then laughed.

I said, "Thanks for coming, but you must respect our time better." He explained that he had to fix a pipe somewhere. "You should tell us that," I said. Calvin then told us that he needed gas now and also needed gas for going into Kingston the next morning. We got to the gas station, and he asked us for money. We gave him JM$3000. He said that he would put JM$2,000 worth of gas in the car and keep the remaining JM$1,000.

Next, we went into Falmouth. We called Sonya, and she was at the Public Works Office. We told her we would meet her at Tasty Patty Place. We ordered patties, bread, and juice. We paid our bill, which came to JM$1,000. The bread was pretty good. I called Dennis, and he said that he was at Duncan's and would call us later or get back to us. We then proceeded to go home to Clark's Town.

Calvin bought a few things, like water and snacks. We reached home at 5:30 p.m., just before it got dark. In Clark's Town, we picked up Georgia, had a snack, and relaxed. The first place we went was the grave sites of Mama, Papa, and Daphne. The path to the site was clean and clear. I missed seeing and talking to Mama, but her spirit was so close. Then we went to the house. We took out the gifts we brought and emptied the suitcases. We only left our clothes. Neville, Dennis, and Andre were thankful for the gifts they received. We proceeded to our bed and set the alarm on our Blackberry for three o'clock the next morning, because we had to leave at four o'clock for Kingston. We ate sandwiches that Georgia prepared.

It was now Saturday morning, October 15, 2011. We left at four o'clock. We had to be in Kingston at King's House by eight o'clock for rehearsal. The road was dark, it was raining, and all the heavy trucks were in front of us. It was raining, and a flood watch warning was on the news. The rain was pouring down as we drove behind two big trailers. Then at full speed, we passed them. We thought, *Great. We'll be in town early.*

When we reached Moneague, the car stopped, and steam was rising from the engine. Calvin popped the hood, and it was steaming. He looked around, but there was no person or house in sight. At this time, it was about 5:45 a.m. Calvin took three bottles of water that we carried with us and put them in the radiator. We then could drive to a more clear and visible spot along the road.

We saw a house that looked like a shop, and then Calvin spotted another house just off the road. He backed into the driveway of that house. Lights were on outside, but inside the house was dark. It appeared that everyone was sleeping. The dogs were barking, but Calvin saw a tank in the yard near the house. He was happy, because if got water, he could drive again. He poured the water into the radiator, and the steam went higher.

"We will have to wait until it cools down," he said. "Maybe another hour." The dogs were barking and coming toward the car. He checked out the dogs; he was so brave. Calvin got out of the car and went into the yard while the dogs were barking. He went too close to the house, and somebody looked out of the house through the window. Calvin called out, and a young man came outside and gave him a container, a bottle to get water from the tank. Then Calvin was able to fill up the water.

Now it was 6:47 a.m. He drove slowly to the town where I could get a taxi to King's House. I saw a car that looked like a taxi at the gas station, but Calvin said it was a police car. He drove and blocked the car and called to the police. The police officer got out of his car, and Calvin recognized him.

"I know the police commander in the police car," Calvin said. "It is Noel. I will ask him if he is going into town, and he can drop you where you can get a cab."

When he spoke to the commander, the commander said, "No problem. I am going into town."

So Stephen and I went into the police car with the commander and the commander's driver. We left Calvin alone at the gas station to sort things out. I said "greetings and good day" to the commander and his driver. We travelled a little way, and then we told him that we were going to King's House so I could receive my Badge of Honour. The commander replied and he was also going there for a Badge of Honour.

I was excited and said, "Oh good!" I introduced him to my hubby Stephen, and then I took my phone out to call Calvin. He said there was a mechanic at the gas station that would get in touch with a friend who knows about radiators. I said to Calvin, "Good! Keep in touch."

Now it was about eight o'clock in the morning, and we were near Kingston in Spanish Town. Calvin was still in the pouring rain in Moneague.

We got to King's House, and the people were under a tent. We ran out of the car into the tent and waited to hear about the instructions regarding the things we had missed. It was so wet that my feet were soaked with water, because I was wearing peep-toed shoes. The organizer, the ambassador, and everyone arranged for us to move into King's House Hall, the governor general's quarters. Only the recipients were allowed in the hall. Therefore, Stephen was not allowed inside. He sat outside in the tent in the cold rain.

I was wearing a summer pantsuit that was very nice and trimmed with a boarder. It was very comfortable for travelling. I had a small travelling bag, which I had to leave with Stephen outside. It was a little bit too big to be in the rehearsal hall. We were seated as per our honour; I was in the third section for Badge of Honour for (Long Service in Religion).

I sat there, and it was so cold. I had been travelling since four o'clock in the morning, and it was now nine thirty. I'd had no food, no tea, and no sleep. I thought of Stephen sitting outside in the cold. I looked around at the staff and workers for the day. I spotted a young man and thought he looked as if I could talk to him. Although we were not allowed to move from our seats, I got up, went over to him, and introduced myself.

"I have been travelling from the country since four o'clock this morning," I explained. "I'm hungry and tired, and my husband is sitting outside in the tent in the rain."

He said, "My name is Learie." I called him Larry. "Leave everything to me," he said, and he went outside. He was so nice. He went for Stephen, who came inside to join us. He had to turn his cell phone off.

I thanked Learie for helping us out. Stephen corrected me and said it was Learie, not Larry. The rehearsal staff and organizers reminded us that inside of the hall was plan B. If it didn't rain on the seventeenth, which was the next day, it would be planned for outside. After I went up when the called my name, I came back to my seat, and Learie took Stephen and myself to get some tea, juice, and patties. We ate and felt better, like we hadn't eaten for days. They were real Jamaican patties.

After we ate, I called Calvin. He was still in the rain. He told us that a mechanic looked at the car and said it would need a new radiator. He added that we would keep in touch. Stephen and I went to the washroom, and it was still raining. We settled down and enjoyed the warmth and the people. A lovely old lady made friends with me. She said she had a basics school in St. Catherine. She was a sweet lady, and we talked all the way, and she was happy to sit beside me. She also got something to eat and drink, and her family was outside waiting. They also finally came inside from the cold. I asked Learie about the photograph to order on Monday, but he told me to not to worry about it and to leave it up to him.

After all was over, it was still raining. I rushed over to see Commander Noel to ask if he could drive us to the Hotel Nutfordcourt. He asked where it was and took us there, and I was so thankful. I went into the lobby, told the front desk that I was early due to my ride, and asked if I could check in early. A young lady said she would see, but a woman beside her said that no rooms were available. She suggested that we go to the restaurant, relax, have something, and check back in two hours. By this time, it was one o'clock in the afternoon.

Stephen and I went to the restaurant and had lunch. It cost us thirty US dollars. My brother thought we were crazy, because it was too expensive. He asked why we hadn't walked up the road. We explained to him that we didn't know where we were and that it was price to pay. Stephen waited and walked. I was tired, so I went to the lobby and rested on the couch. When two hours had passed, I went to the front desk, but the lady and the gentleman said together, "No, no, no, no room." It was now two o'clock, and check-in time was three o'clock. We slept on the couch.

I called Calvin, and he said he was now at Bogwalk. He told me that Oliver would come to us for money to buy a gastric something for the car. I gave him JM$6,000 Jamaican, and that was all we had. Oliver said he had to buy the part and then take it to Calvin at Bogwalk. He said he was far away, so I prayed. Oliver came for the money sometime between four and five o'clock. Calvin was in Linstead, so they left the van at Linstead where Oliver had towed the car to a police station. Oliver drove Calvin to the hotel where we were.

When Calvin arrived, he was tired and wet. He got his hair cut and shaved by Stephen, and he rested. It was now seven o'clock. Dennis called and said he would be up Sunday evening by eight o'clock. The night was wet, and Oliver came to be with Calvin in Portmore. Stephen and I rested until Sunday morning. Sunday morning we slept in and then went down to the restaurant and had a good breakfast. Calvin called and informed us that the car could not be fixed, because it was Sunday and everybody was at church.

We went back to our hotel room where I called my cousin Ceta and my girlfriend Vivia. Vivia was coming to see me at eleven o'clock that morning. She came and forgot my room number. She waited for a while, and then the front desk called me and we went down to get her. It was now noon.

It was so nice to see her, and we chatted. She could not stay with us for lunch, but she told us about Island Grill up the road. Calvin was going to meet us there with Oliver at one o'clock. Well, at breakfast, Stephen was not focused on anything. He went along, looking at the restaurant, the place, and the women at the front desk. I called to him and let him know that we had to discuss the day and what we had to spend. He was very relaxed, but I was concerned about Calvin and what was to happen next.

Vivia dropped us off at Island Grill, and Calvin was there waiting. We sat and ate. We ordered soup, rice, and peas—real Jamaican food. We had pumpkin rice, callaloo rice, and nice fruit juices, which was not expensive. At dinner, we suggested we go look for Aunt Iris and cousin Ceta. Oliver suggested we walk back and enjoy Independence Square. He had to go, so Calvin, Stephen, and I walked to Independence Park, which is a beautiful park. We took pictures and walked back to the hotel.

By this time, Calvin had communicated with the mechanic about his car and found out he wouldn't get it back until Monday or Tuesday. Oliver was going to pick him up after the awards on Monday to get it fixed. Calvin was so tired after we came back to the hotel at four o'clock. I waited for Oliver to take me to see Ceta, but he didn't show up. I was disappointed and so was Ceta. Stephen, Calvin, and I watched TV, chatted, and waited for Dennis to show up. Then he came and took us to Island Grill. We walked to Island Grill, because we said it was near. He was fuming, because the walk was too long. We walked back at a quicker pace. He took Calvin, and they left. We all decided that Rosie, my cousin-in-law, would meet us all there to go to King's House.

The next day was October 17. It was the big day. Stephen and I decided to get ready and head down to the restaurant for breakfast. Breakfast was not ready until 6:30 a.m. At 6:30 a.m., we went back to check, but breakfast was not ready. We had to go to King's House, and it was now 6:45. We picked up a coffee.

Dennis, Rosie, Calvin, Stephen, and I got into Rosie's jeep, and I placed my VIP sticker on her dashboard. As we reached King's House, they were setting up the guards, the army, and the policemen to receive recipients and guests. We asked where to park and ended up parking beside the general secretary to the ambassador. She said hello and went on to talk to Rosie. Rosie was excited to see her. Rosie said she had been her French teacher, so they knew each other.

We walked over to the tent where the awardees and family were to sit. We looked on the names to see where they were supposed to sit, and then I went over to look on the names to see where I would be sitting. Then I saw Learie. I gave him the forty Jamaican dollars for the Jamaica Information Service to get the pictures that would be taken of me during the ceremony. Stephen took my camera and began taking pictures all over the place. The scenery was great.

I met Dale, the former counsel for Canada, and we took pictures. Then Vivia came in, the former counsel general for Canada, and we took more pictures. We hugged and laughed, and then we were all seated. It was now nine o'clock.

The program started with the guard of honours march, the police defense staff, the guard commander salutes, leader of the opposition, the prime minister, and his Excellency the Governor General and all the other dignitaries. Next, the ceremony of investiture and presentation of the National Honours and Awards 2011 commenced. The ground was still wet, but it was sunny. The ladies beside me were very upset that the sun was shining on them, so they were moving closer behind me. Everyone was from different parts of the Jamaica, Canada, the United States, and the United Kingdom.

The ladies behind me were a bit annoying, because they were talking nonstop throughout the ceremony. I got up at one point and stood off to the side. But all in all, most of the people were courteous and nice. Then it was time for me to go up for my honour. I was calm, very proud, very serene, and prayerful. I went up and stood at the first guard, then the second guard, and the third guard before going up to the Governor General, where I bowed and received my handshake, badge, and scroll. There were lots of pictures taken. I got a cup of tea and went back to my seat.

After the ceremony, everyone was rushing to get pictures with the prime minister. When I realised that, I rushed to get a few pictures as well. I always went to get pictures with the opposition and all the people around. We took pictures and then greeted each other and proceeded to the van where we all went in and discussed where we were going to have lunch. We decided we would go to Iron Pot.

At this time, my feet were sore, and I felt as if my shoes were coming off my feet. My legs were tired, but I was still in awe. We drove to Iron Pot, and I noticed the bottoms of my shoes were wet and the soles were coming off. I decided that I would stay focused, have a good meal, and get back to the hotel. We sat and ate lunch; I had curry goat and a nice cup of soup.

After the wonderful meal, Rosie drove us back to the hotel where I changed and then checked out at 1:30 p.m. We put our luggage in Dennis's van, because he was going to drive us back to the country in Clark's Town. Oliver came for Calvin, and they both went to get the car at Linstead to tow it to the garage. It was quite nice driving down; it did not rain. On our way down, Dennis stopped at a breadfruit festival, but not much was going on. He then proceeded to his farmhouse in Brampton to look after the goats. We waited for him for an hour. We finally got to Clark's Town at 5:45 p.m.

We picked up Georgia who had been walking home. The night was short, and we got a lot of rest because we were tired. Neville came up to the house to talk about the award and stayed with us for a while. We prayed for safe travel back, and Stephen began packing for our trip the next day.

It was now Tuesday morning, October 18. I woke at six o'clock that morning, and Stephen got up at seven. We prayed and had porridge, green banana, and fried dumplings. Calvin was still in Kingston waiting for a miracle. Calvin's car was not ready, so Dennis called and took us to the airport. We then proceeded to drop Stephen off at the airport by midday.

I stayed with Dennis for the rest of the day while he drove around and did his work. It was relaxing but different. He stopped at a site where they were building a Claremont and then stopped at Falmouth William K Nibb School where I met the principal and took pictures. I am an alumnus. I was very pleased to see the renovations and noticed that the six grade colours had changed.

All day I was in and out of the car. Dennis took me for lunch at the markets in the arcades where Naaman had a bar and restaurant. I got a bottle of Ting juice and a fish dinner. The food was a large portion and spicy, but I ate some. Dennis ordered chicken, and we both asked for takeout. My sister Cecile came down and saw me. She hugged and greeted me and then said that she'd seen me on TV.

Next, I went to the digital place to check my minutes, and I had a lot left. Dennis was rushing to go, so we left and went to pick up his trailer that men were working on. When we were done, we went back to the school where I met my nephew O'Neil and took pictures with him. Now, I was getting really tired. Dennis stopped at Duncan's where I bought bread and drinks that cost JM$1,600.

Stephen called and said he was boarding the plane and was off to Canada. After a long day with Dennis, we got home at six o'clock, and Georgia was on her way home too. Dennis left for the night, and I ate some more food that was left, chicken and rice. I was so tired that I went to bed early and slept like a baby. Stephen called to say that he arrived safely in Toronto and was getting ready for work the next day.

That Wednesday morning I got up fresh and nice. Georgia went off to work, and I was left alone with two Rottweiler-Dobermans. I walked around the estate, picking pears and June plums. Neville came up to the home, and I gave him JM$1,000 to buy chicken or fish and rice to cook for dinner. George left the dried peas, so I put them in the pot to soak. Neville made up the fire outside. Neville came back and said that the chicken was too expensive, so he brought back fish. Then I seasoned and fried the fish inside the house, while he soaked the peas outside the house. It was now the afternoon, and I relaxed and walked around the house.

The dogs came out, and I realised they were really hungry, so I went inside and called Calvin to tell him the dogs were outside and hungry. He said the car couldn't be fixed that day, so he had to get a ride down, but he would feed the dogs. Calvin came in with rice and roast breadfruit, and we sat and had a luscious meal. Calvin rushed out to do business with the driver. Dennis came back up to the house and stayed there for the night. Georgia and her sons came in and ate, and Calvin and Dennis went to pay their respects to a deceased family member and did not return until one o'clock the next morning. Dennis slept in the front room and left early in the morning for work. I was ready to go to my bed and relax.

The next morning was the final morning of my stay in Jamaica. It was Thursday morning at six o'clock. I woke up, did my devotion, and felt good. I spoke to Vivia and Daddy in Linstead and then called Toronto before having breakfast. Again, I had roasted breadfruit, banana, and callaloo. When I was done, I repacked my suitcase.

Calvin came in, because he was going to be travelling to Toronto with me, and he packed. Dennis came for us both at ten o'clock, and we proceeded to Falmouth. Calvin picked up documents from a businessman, we proceeded to Montego Bay, and Calvin did business in Montego Bay. By noon, we were on our way to the airport. Calvin and I bought lunch duty-free, and we boarded flight 2703 at 2:25 p.m. We sat beside each other in seats 7d and 7e and had a smooth flight all the way to Toronto, where we landed at seven o'clock.

I unlocked my phone and switched it back to Toronto. I called Stephen to tell him we had landed safely. By 7:30 p.m., we had picked up our luggage, and Stephen picked us up by eight o'clock. It was a cool 9 degrees Celsius but pleasant. It was nice to be home.

Stephen cooked up a storm. We ate and were ready for bed. Before we retired to bed, we called home to Dennis, Georgia, Naaman, and Clover. We were all pleasantly relaxing. I clicked on my e-mail and knew what I had to do for the next day, so I put everything in order. We went to bed by 10:30 p.m. and were ready for reality the next day.

It was Friday morning, and reality set in. There were phone calls to make, e-mails to answer, and youth entrepreneur work to be done back in the office. I tell you all these true stories so that you can understand that life can change at any time. One day you are in Japan and the next you're in Jamaica, but life goes on. I'm looking forward to a nice holiday on the beach. As you read this book, may it enlighten your path of life to realize that moments and time changes and so do people. I miss back ah yawd.

MOMENTS OF SHARING

I HAVE BEEN IN ministry for more than thirty-six years and have lived in Canada for more than forty years. My first son is thirty-four, and my second is twenty-nine; both are married. I have five grandchildren, three girls and two boys. I really enjoy them. I enjoyed my family coming over for summertime barbecues, cooking Sunday meals, and having friends over for tea. My oldest grandchildren, Smai and Jasiri, stayed over on weekends unless I had functions to go to. My three youngest are Omari, a boy, and two princesses, one is Jasmine and the other India. They have been a great addition my family.

Every December 26, family, friends, and members of the congregation join me at home for a festive feast. I have great people in the church, both young and faithful, and a great choir. I do a lot of home visits after Sunday service to be with members and get more acquainted with everyone.

One of the most exciting moments was the election time in my riding. One of the candidates was one of the brothers in our community. We were run off our feet, dropping off flyers, making signs, and making phone calls. This was one of my personal civic duties as a citizen.

I spent most of my early mornings and nights reading and writing proposals for funding for the youth organization. I always do a lot of research and reading. I love books; reading to me is very relaxing, and the knowledge I gain from other authors is credited in my own writing. I love literature so much. During my high school days, I always had As in that course. Now my early morning devotions keep me through the day, and my exercise on the treadmill gives me the boost to go the extra mile.

I would not be able to write proposals without the help of Ms K. She is a beautiful, intelligent, and bright young woman who always knows how to stay focused. She was dedicated to my organization and also held the passion to work with youth and the community.

This is my typical day: I wake up at 5:30 a.m. for devotion until 6:00 a.m., and then I exercise until 7:00 a.m. I then prepare fruits for breakfast, and after breakfast, I get ready and go on the computer and make various calls on my priority list in my daily planner. I attend functions and meetings. I work all day, either with the youth, in my office at home, or at the church. Lunch for me is quiet for prayer time. I either have lunch inside or outside and always with a few friends. Sometimes my friends take me out for lunch.

After a full day, I do quiet meditation if I am not having a group meditation session. Then I drive home, cook, and have a meal, which always consists of vegetables, rice, or rice and peas. Prayer time is at 9:00 p.m. when I turn off my phone. After prayer time, I either read or write, depending on what is due at the time.

Even when my youngest son was still living at home, I was alone most of the time. People sometimes asked whether I felt lonely or not. The truth is I never had a sense of loneliness. I do not know what it is to feel lonely, because I have always found happiness in what I do. I've been blessed with a passion to work and help anyone in need who passes my way.

During my days of writing and making contracts, I met a lot of people in different areas of service in Canada. I met Member of Parliament s, Member of Provincial Parliament s, and wonderful people in the banking system and real estate. I changed my accountant in 2004, and that was the best thing I had ever done. He was a great accountant but needed to be reliable. I joined various corporations and became a member of various associations. The Lawyer's Association was great, and I got the chance to meet great lawyers at charities and agencies who gave lectures and training on how to run a successful not-for-profit organization.

Let me say this: with a charitable organization, I learned fast to dot all my *I*s and cross all my *T*s. I arranged for a lady to come into my office and key all of my bookkeeping work and make sure everything was in place. She travelled far to the other end of the city just to set up my office. I am now blessed with an accounting system that works for both the government and the organization.

During my childhood, I was taught to be honest in all that I do. My dad's exact words were "Do well, act good, do not lie, and do not create problems. When you go to bed, you must be able to sleep and know you have a clear conscience." I live by these words.

During the celebration for my twenty-fifth year in ministry, someone asked me, "What makes you so successful?"

I said, "A free mind, a free heart flowing with love."

Another question I got was, "Do you get angry?"

"Yes," I answered, "but I handle my anger with calmness."

"How can you do that?"

"I transcend all personal feelings and interpretations. I embrace self-actualization and focus on the results ahead," I explained.

Someone also asked, "How do you show your affection to your children and others?"

"I carry my affection at home with joy," I said. "I have boundaries but show the affection with me, although I am human."

"How do you cultivate such a presence?"

"I meditate day and night, I exercise, eat well, look into the mirror and say 'Deloris, you are beautiful; you look good.' I do not wait for compliments. I give them to myself first," I said.

"How do you make decisions daily?" another person asked.

"Life is a school," I said. "I'm always learning. What you put in, you get out. I learn every day, I teach every day. Success comes from within; the Super Being, the Creator, is the source I tap into."

Daily:

- I grow.
- I work.
- I love.
- I have children.
- I live.
- I travel.
- I go to school.
- I study the word of God.
- I pray.
- I laugh.
- I run.
- I dance.
- I give high praise to the Almighty God.
- I keep great friends, mostly men and faithful women friends, who always last for many years.

I am a spiritual teacher, and I use this gift to make a difference. I treat everyone as human beings. I love others and everything around me. Thanks be to God!

People think different things about the person they think they know—her Grace Archbishop, Deloris, Dr. Seiveright, and (going way back to the seventies) Mother Dell, or just D, a mother to all. Church members vary in thought, and these are their comments: "She is strict, a fun person when you get to know her, very knowledgeable, kind, loving, and honest. She will tell you as she sees it (straight up). Her eyes are like an owl; you cannot fool her, maybe for a while but not for long. She is faithful, works hard, and the list goes on."

The latest quote from notes that have been given to me, tells the tale. "A special prayer for you, Archbishop. From Psalm 16:11, saying: I have shown path of life, and Archbishop will live in the peace and fullness of joy. Archbishop, the help you give others, the busy year ahead may our saviour, with humble prayer, bless you and keep you in his loving care."

Someone else wrote: "We know you are everything to us, we wish you everything that will make your spirit sing, your heart happy, your age's beautiful. We love you."

Josiah: "Mom, thank you for praying for the blessing for your love. A beautiful mother is what you have always been to me. Friendship that is never failing, for her eyes that see the best in me and her gentle wisdom that carries me through, for her prayers that lift me up, and the dreams she holds in her heart for me. For her smiles and hugs we share, I am forever grateful. I am so thankful to God for entrusting me to the love of the world's most wonderful mother."

This quote is from a lady, and it starts: "You birth me spiritually as a mother, although not biological."

This quote is from a great family member: "May your days be filled with love, blessings, and happiness you so deeply deserve." These words were touching to me, as I share them, I'm sure you can understand why.

Another friend wrote: "You're such a good example of God's love at work in the world. It shows in the kind words that you say and the thoughtfulness toward others. The words given by you, Archbishop, are so great for my life and ministry. May you have faith to inspire, hope to sustain, and love to bless you."

As my readers, may you also be blessed by these words. As I share these wonderful thoughts, I am sure your family and friends and all your community can emulate these virtues.

TESTIMONIALS

"[Deloris] is a strong, spiritual gift and creation from God. She is a light that shines through every individual. The thing as a person that impresses me is strong morality, which is not only kept for herself and immediate family, but shares it and lives it. She's not only a preacher, but teacher no matter what age. Blessings be with you always."   ~ Sister Joyce.

"Archbishop is a very powerful woman influence in my life. Archbishop gives me a very peaceful feeling. I could listen to her praying every day."
~ Linda

"Deloris is a very inspirational person. She is like a magnet in the Spirit. She is [a] natural leader who is willing to lead in any path, but the righteous path. She is a lady of wisdom. She is a down-to-earth person. She is a person of valour. Christ lives within her at all times. There are a lot of good words that could describe Deloris, but the best description is that she is a good person and [a] godly person."   ~ Late Bob

"Archbishop is a very caring, loving person. She is very kind when she gives it from her heart. She is the kind of person you would want for a mother, strict but gentle, cares about your well-being, as if one of her own child[ren]. She is a person you can only be mad at for a minute. To some, she is the kind of person I believe God is pleased with. Arch, I love you. I always will."   ~ Sharon W.

"Archbishop Deloris is very motherly and caring. She has a positive attitude that attracts you to her. She is an excellent listener and great advisor. She is the type of person you feel that you know for a long time even after a five-minute conversation. Elle est une mere a nowstous qui aime sans limite. Elle a une troisieme sense rien un secret. Elle peu lire tes pense alors tu peu rien cacher. Une vrai mere."   ~ P.C.

"Meeting Deloris has been an inspiration. The level of integrity and compassion for youth have inspired me to be more thoughtful to people. Upon meeting her, I felt she was more of a mother to me and others around her. Any word of advice she gives us is always welcome. I must say, I love her style. She is always dressed nicely with beautiful life. Deloris a truly a mother to all with style."   ~ Sandra

"She's a teacher, knowledgeable, articulate, compassionate, considerate, calming, influential, and insightful. Always prepared to help, she will surprise you, always reading about everything. She is tactful, very resourceful, and always thinking about the community at large. I have seen the joy and respect by others that have been blessed by being in her presence. She is committed to all her causes. As they say, the hardest working woman in the show business. She has blessed me and many others, and I hope she will continue. God Bless Dr. Deloris Seiveright."   ~ Justine

"To me, Archbishop Deloris is many wonderful things. She is a kind spirit that was sent through divine interaction. She is a mother that shows concern for all my well-being. She is a friend to chat and laugh with. She is a mentor who has taught me and opened doors of opportunity through my ordination into her ministry. She has shown me that my possibilities are bondless and the strength through spirit."   ~ Paula

"I met Archbishop in 1998, It Old Years Night, and I attended her service. My first impression of her was that she was spirit-filled. After her sermon, I was edified, alert, conscious, and blessed."   ~ C. Webb

"Deloris is a friend, one that I have utter confidence and trust. I am blessed to have a friend that I can be totally honest with and not feel that I am being judged. That doesn't mean that she can't share her thoughts and her honesty apart from what she truly sees. When I am with Deloris, I feel as if I'm with my sister and her family. It's a delight to sit in her kitchen and share a meal, both admiring and teasing her sons at the same time."
                    ~ Sharon

"My name is Ivan Mentor, and today I am writing in this book about a woman that is one of the greatest women I have come across. Why? Because she is always there when I need her, winter, summer, whatever he weather. Her name is Deloris Devan Seiveright; that is a leader. But as a spiritual mother, she is known as the Archbishop Dr. Deloris Seiveright. I have known her most of my life in Canada and her book named *Thoughts and Prayers from the Heart* should be read by everyone. My family and I love her. May God bless her today, tomorrow, and forever."   ~ Ivan Mentor

"My life has been a journey of roadblocks and tribulations. Since I met the Archbishop, you and God have been my guiding light through the rough times. Thank you for beings so understanding, and thank you for believing in vision and dreams. I will no doubt be keeping in touch with you. I won't let you down, along with myself. I [am] so glad that God has blessed you with a gift of guidance and a loving heart. You will always have a place in my heart and my life. Please keep me on my toes and direct me straight to my times of despair."   ~ A.R. (A youth)

"Thank you for everything. Thank you for making me into a blue-collar businessman. Because [of] this program, I had dreams. Now I have a mission and goals. Thank you very much sincerely."   ~ R.G. (youth)

"Thank you for everything that you have done for me. Without this program, I would have been working at a factory or a fast-food restaurant by now. This program has shown me a lot about becoming my own boss and being successful in life."   ~ N.O. (youth)

"Archbishop, I want you to know that you are a beautiful soul. From the day I met you to the last moment your spirit rise. Everyone around me feels it, every second and brightens their day. You inspire me. Thank You."
                    ~ N.N. (youth)

ABOUT THE AUTHOR

Her Grace Archbishop Dr. Deloris Seiveright M.Msc. BH(L)

Archbishop Dr. Deloris Seiveright is the founder and archbishop of the Shouters National Evangelical Spiritual Baptist Faith International Centre of Canada (NESBF), overseer of the Canadian Archdiocese, and cofounder of one of the first Spiritual Baptist churches in Toronto, St. Frederic's Cathedral. A distinguished member of the Caribbean Religious Community, the Archbishop has not limited her time and contributions to her church alone, but has also provided a community service in Ontario and abroad. She is a recipient of awards like the African Canadian Achievement Award and the Racial Harmony Award, as well as leadership awards from Toronto Victims Service and Shouters NESBF. Her latest honour was the Prime Minister Office of Jamaica Badge of Honour for Long Service in Religion BH(L). Dr. Seiveright's vision, enthusiasm, and leadership skills are exemplified through her longstanding years of volunteer work and accomplishment.

She has been ordained since 1978 and has been a licensed minister in the province of Ontario since 1984. She earned a diploma in business administration from Ryerson University in Toronto and an honorary doctorate in theology from St. Andrew Theology Seminary in London. She has received a bachelor's degree in religious education from Tyndale

Seminary and a master's degree in metaphysical science from the International University of Metaphysics in Arizona. She is a certified counsellor in general, youth, and family; and has her certificate of multifaith competency from Ontario Multifaith Council.

Her work empowers youth and builds their future with love for the betterment of the community. She has developed and implemented youth mentorship, entrepreneurial, and crime-prevention programs. She serves and mentors youth, building their self-esteem through her coaching of respect, spiritual awareness, honesty, and humanity. She also provides youth employment opportunities and has launched a scholarship fund to assist youth with their education.

Her service is not limited to youth alone. As an archbishop and an overseer of several churches, with her strong African Canadian traditions and Spiritual Baptist Christian beliefs, she is able to be involved in helping to solve community problems and issues. She serves on various boards, feeds those in need, visits the ill, gives guidance, and heads special projects that celebrate the International Year of Older Persons.

An evangelist at heart, the Archbishop speaks from the heart at churches, conferences, seminars, and workshops. She works to demystify the misconceptions surrounding Spiritual Baptists and Christianity. She communicates through lectures, various media, TV, and radio programs. She is strong believer in studying to show oneself approved and an accomplished academic. She enjoys music and meditation and has authored three self-published books. However, she loves most of all to preach and teach the word of God.